How to Develop New Products
for Sale to Industry

How to Develop New Products for Sale to Industry

Frank M. Butrick

Prentice-Hall, Inc.
Englewood Cliffs, N.J.

PRENTICE-HALL INTERNATIONAL, INC., *London*
PRENTICE-HALL OF AUSTRALIA, PTY. LTD., *Sydney*
PRENTICE-HALL OF CANADA, LTD., *Toronto*
PRENTICE-HALL OF INDIA PRIVATE LTD., *New Delhi*
PRENTICE-HALL OF JAPAN, INC., *Toyko*

© 1971 BY
PRENTICE-HALL, INC.
ENGLEWOOD CLIFFS, N. J.

Library of Congress
Catalog Card Number: 74-145627

PRINTED IN THE UNITED STATES OF AMERICA
ISBN–0-13-405001-0
B&P

About the Author

Frank M. Butrick operates his own consulting practice, devoted to guiding business in successful new-product ventures. His broad-gauged experience includes high level positions with a variety of industrial firms whose products range from furniture to plumbing goods.

The author's systematic approach to new-product development has been put to the test as he has been responsible for setting up new-product development departments, product screening activities, idea evaluation procedures – every new-product activity from idea through production to distribution. Most recently, he developed a pilot plant for making a specialized industrial product and sold the firm to National Twist Drill and Tool Company, a division of Lear Siegler, Inc.

An active writer for twenty years, Mr. Butrick is the author of hundreds of articles for business, trade, and professional magazines. He is also a popular speaker and instructor before manufacturing, engineering, and marketing audiences.

How This Book Helps You Plan and Produce New Products That Sell

This book is a working manual for the successful development, introduction, and management of new products—specifically those intended for sale to industry or to businesses. Unfortunately, in spite of almost universal activity in new-product development, the procedure has an astonishingly poor success record. Statistics reported by various authorities differ (mostly because no one defines either success or failure), but it is clear that the average odds for a new industrial product accomplishing its twin goals of achieving a significant share of the market and worthwhile profits are only about 1 in 20! One is tempted to sweep these findings under the carpet of some convenient phrase, such as "most new-product failures do not meet the needs of the market." But that just will not do, since examples are legion of two or more firms introducing essentially similar products, with widely divergent levels of financial success. So one arrives at an indisputable conclusion: in the vast majority of cases, the difference—the only difference—between new-product success and failure is management—the way in which each firm handles the selection, development, introduction, and volume-building stages of its new products.

The purpose of this book is to examine the pitfalls that beset new-product development, and then show how to avoid them; how to select, plan, and manage new products to obtain satisfactory levels of market penetration and profits. It is meant to be a guide for all those who become involved within the firm—not to show them how to perform their jobs, but to show them how to integrate their activities with those of other departments, within the overall development project goals.

But most of all, this book is meant as a working manual for the man who fulfills the function of new-product manager, whatever his actual title may be. And since deliberate, planned new-product development is a relatively new concept, this book is primarily written for the neophyte—not as an attempt to make him an overnight expert, but to help him become a competent and consistent contributor to the profits and longevity of the firm.

The future of any firm depends, to a large degree, upon the success of its new-product ventures. Men who become experienced in successful new-product development will find their role becoming of ever-increasing importance as technology and the tempo of business continue their always accelerating pace. This book is for such men—to help them get started and avoid learning through expensive trial and error; to help make the odds on new-product development more equitable.

HOW THIS BOOK IS ORGANIZED

How to Develop New Products for Sale to Industry is not a book of general principles or of concepts drawn against the broad spectrum of American business. It is a working book, with the focus drawn sharply upon manufactured products sold to men who buy upon behalf of their employers—sales to industry, construction, and other businesses as opposed to the individual consumer or mass market. It is written for the manager of new products—the man (whatever his title or other duties) who is responsible for overseeing the development, introduction, and early sales of new products.

Like Gaul, the book is divided into three parts. The first deals with the new-product development *function,* and the second with new-product development *operation.* In the third are detailed treatments of specific subjects and departments which become involved in new-product *development.*

Section I. It is essential that there be careful planning for the structure and operation of the new-product development function. Haphazard product development has an abysmal record. If a company hopes to achieve worthwhile new-product success, it must organize for the work involved. This means establishing corporate goals and criteria, setting up a new-product development staff (or man), and working out effective operating procedures. Four chapters cover organizing for new products, where it fits in the chain of command, putting the right man in charge, and getting started.

Section II. There are three classes of new products, each class involving progressively greater work, lead time, investment, and risk. This section has three chapters, each a detailed step-by-step manual for the successful development of a class of new products. Used together, they cover the entire path—from new idea conception to profitable maturity in the market place.

Section III. The manager of new-product development cannot hope to be expert in every phase of such a complex activity. From his own experience he will have considerable knowledge of some areas, an acquaintance with others, and ignorance of a few. This section is for helping him fill in the gaps—introducing the marketing man to production, the engineer to selling, the salesman to patents, and generally for passing on some of the hard-won fruits of the author's experience.

Frank M. Butrick

Table of Contents

How to Develop New Products
for Sale to Industry

SECTION I

The New - Product Development Function

Chapter 1

19:1--The Odds Against You

> . . . and how to organize so that the odds are more equitable. Your firm has developed new products before—but how many of them have provided the profits that were anticipated? This chapter spells out the corporate climate necessary for long-term profitable new-product development—and how easy it is to improve your new-product success ratio.

YOU CANNOT AVOID NEW PRODUCTS

Almost every company is now doing new-product development, either constantly or sporadically. This is natural for a corporation. The problem with the majority of new products is that they are not developed—they are let grow. This lack of thinking, planning, and deliberation produces the miserable track record for new-product development. In 1968, over $500 million was spent to launch 6500 new products.* Some 85% were complete failures and another 9% were unrewarding. Statistically, if your company develops 20 new products, only one will be profitable enough to justify the effort. Worse yet, most of the other 19 will lose money—not because they were bad ideas—but because they were so mishandled that they never had a chance!

Any new product is much too important to a company to be left to grow—to sink or swim—of its own accord. The entire future of your company may well depend upon how successfully you develop new products. Is the statement too strong? Well, perhaps you have a product line that simply does not change much with the years, such as hammer handles—or do hammer handles change? It appears as though wooden hammer handles are being challenged by concoctions of metal and plastic. Pick another

*This interesting statistic was reported by Paul Field, senior editor, *Business Management,* in "Why New Products Marketing Is So Tough," July 1969. It includes consumer products and is thus misleading for industrial products—which are probably worse.

example, something really steady, like lathe tool bits. Yet comparing a modern tool-bit catalog with one dated 1900, we find everything changed except the appearance—way back then tool bits were carbon tool-steel, while today practically all cutting tools are high-speed steel (developed around World War I) or carbide (developed around World War II). How about carpet tacks? Nope—being displaced by staples. Hand files! Got me—but name one major maker of files who has found it unnecessary to diversify through new-product development. In short, even an industry which does not change is constantly changing, constantly developing, constantly coming out with new products—and facing 19:1 odds.

And clinging to a safe, old-time product becomes more risky every year. If you look at a turn-of-the-century mail-order catalog you will find that 75% of the products are no longer made—or have changed or altered so much as to be recognizable in a generic sense only. There are only a handful of products in an old catalog that even retain their appearance after the passage of 6 decades. There is no safety in retrenchment. You grow up or drift down.

So put the cards squarely on the table:

1. 50 years from now, 75% of the products you make today will be obsolete, radically different, or under heavy pressure from someone else's new product.
2. A third of the products you will be making 50 years from now have not yet been thought of. Another third will be copies of new products developed by other companies.
3. Your only corporate salvation during the next 5 decades is new-product development—yet statistically the odds are 19:1 against your being able to develop a single profitable new product!

Of course, 50 years is a long time. The author and most of the readers of this book were not alive 50 years ago and will not be alive 50 years from now. So why worry? But assume a linear relationship; crystal ball only 10 years away, 120 months. Not at all far away. Within that brief span nearly 20% of the products you make today will be obsolete or vastly altered! Nearly 10% of the products which you will be selling 10 years hence you have not yet thought of—or at least not thought about. And your chances are still only 1 in 19 of developing a profitable new product!

Ho-hum? Put it this way: if management men in their 40's today hope to retire from their present employer at age 60, the chances are about 1 in 4 that product failures and obsolescence will not have left a company from which to retire! Men entering business today, fresh from accounting, engineering and management courses in college, are busily joining companies which may not even exist 20 years hence! Reread your employee retirement program. How valuable would it be to you if the company did not exist? Of if the division where you work is closed out?

Talk to any executive who has been with the company more than 10 years and ask him what products were introduced during his time. It is certain that his list will be surprisingly long—and even more certain that, if complete, it will include many badly mangled sales opportunities and very few real successes. One manufacturer made a thorough survey of his existing products in relation to their market penetration and sales potential. He discovered that if the products introduced during the last 10 years had been better managed, the firm's sales volume today would be nearly 100% greater! That is much too high a price to pay for lack of planning, for lack of new-product development.

This new-product development process is vastly too important to leave to chance. Or to leave to somebody to attend to when he has time. It is too important to leave to production, who are busy with today's problem of getting goods out. You cannot leave it to sales, who are preoccupied with getting new customers, keeping the present ones, and complaining about delivery. Even R&D cannot help; they are fascinated by the R, neglect the D, and know nothing of marketing anyway.

New-product management is much too important to be left to chance. Its importance demands that the chief executive give the subject the thought which it deserves and that he green-light procedures to maximize his company's chances of success.

THE STATISTICS SPELL MISMANAGEMENT

Manufacturing is a remarkably healthy business. It has to be, just to survive—because, in many ways, manufacturing is almost unbelievably inefficient. In any company this can quickly be seen by an outsider—new employee, consultant, service man, etc. Why do we insiders not see our inefficiencies? Because we are used to them. Buy a new house and you make a long mental list of things that absolutely must be fixed. Six months later, most of them are not—and never will be. Why? Because they are no longer bothersome. Familiarity breeds tolerance—eventually, a sort of approval.

The president, hearing no high-pitched screams of anguish, assumes that all is well. He knows that *most* decisions are right, *most* products work, *most* shipments are on time, and the firm makes money *most* years. So what can be wrong? Obviously, anything that is not right *most* of the time.

And in one specific area—a vital one—American manufacturing management chalks up a score that is worse than deliberate fumbling: new-product development as a profit-building activity. According to often-published statistics, over 8 out of every 10 new industrial products fail. If anything, this is highly optimistic. But no such statistic can be accurate, because nobody bothers to define "failure." A little company's catastrophe is a big company's inconvenience, quickly covered up. But after 15 years in and around new-product development, the author can cite hundreds of new-product histories that add up about like this:

> 60% resulted in a money loss
> 30% about broke even, without significant loss but without profit from the
> work involved
> 8% were profitable but provided a disappointingly low return—the money
> should have been invested in some other project
> 2% paid off well, handsomely, or fantastically

Regardless of whose opinion—or statistic—is employed, all agree, as shown in Figure 1-1, that new-product development has a poor track record.

New-product development, as practiced today, is a corporate indoor sport, not a

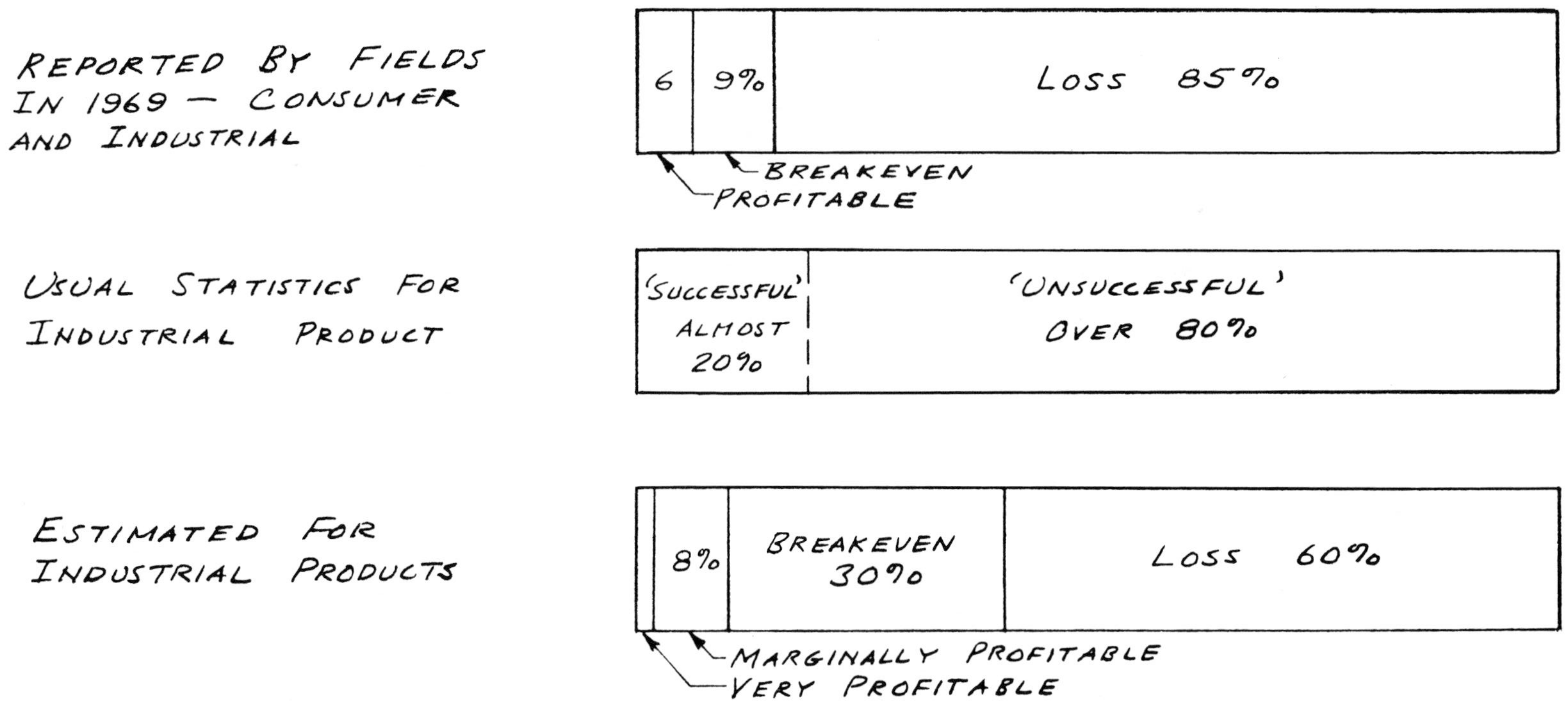

Figure 1-1

It is impossible to pin down the statistics for new-product success—partly because nobody defines success. The difference between success and failure is not a sharp line; it is a blurred area, with disappointing profits on the top and modest losses (usually rationalized with "We needed it to fill out our line," or " to open a new market," etc.) on the bottom. The graph shows comparative estimates of American industry's batting average.

management activity. It is a treasure hunt, approached with the same logic, planning, executive skill, and results that would be demonstrated if management invested in sweepstake tickets. And this should not be, because it need not be.

What is needed? A deliberate effort. If not a grand master plan, then at least the same forethought that is put into maintaining the factory roof, or keeping the office lawn well tended. In short, a goal is needed. A vision of what might be, of what can be if it is desired enough to work for it.

New-product ideas are a dime a dozen. Good ones, too. But what is rare is a concerted, deliberate, planned program of making a new product a fully developed member of the profit-carrying product line. If management cannot visualize a good new product five years away, when it has achieved significant stature in the product line, then it must listen to those who can. Because that is what is missing—an accurate picture of what a new product can become in sales, profits, and improved market position. Once this picture, this forecast, is sharply in focus, then it is a relatively simple matter to determine how to get it there. What production capacity is needed, and when. What inventory build up is needed, and when the money will be invested. How the product will be introduced to the market, and how much heavy sales and promotion pressure is needed to achieve an accelerated growth rate.

Once a clear definition of the end of the journey has been established, then the route, or alternate routes, can be plotted with relative certainty. And if top management and all others concerned have the goal sharply in mind, the new product will not be lost in the shuffle, will not become forgotten, nor run over by day-to-day emergencies. And that is exactly what happens to most new-product ventures; they die on the vine from malnutrition. To be sure, some are no good to start with, some are dreamed up as a result of warped marketing notions, and some just do not work as expected. But most new products are left on the doorstep of the sales department—foundlings. Like results of unplanned parenthood, the new products are loved temporarily until they misbehave or demand more than their share of time and effort. Then they are pushed into the corner, to be seen but not heard from and eventually they are no longer seen. Since they contribute little if any profit to the corporation, creeping neglect sets in. Are these products "failures"? Yes. Utter failures are killed off, and show up in the statistics. *But any product which does not achieve a significant market penetration, or contribute an important share to the corporate sales volume, or accomplish that which could logically be expected of it, is a failure.* It is a waste of good men's time, efforts, and energy; a waste of the corporation's funds, better left in interest-paying investments.

Then what is a new-product success? Any product, not now being sold, which is added to the product line and over a period of a few years produces:

1. A significant increase in the corporation's total sales volume.
2. A significant penetration into its own market.
3. Profits in line with other products.
4. Reasonably fast (3-5 years) return on all developmental and introductory costs.
5. Shows reasonable life expectancy.

6. Does well enough to reward its champions with satisfaction and to encourage them to try a new one.

And this can only result from a carefully followed agreed-upon master plan, which in turn is derived from an intelligent market research program and from new products developed to fulfill market opportunities or developed in conjunction with market feedback. Thus, new-product development (see Figure 1-2), is a time-consuming process, spread over a number of years, which involves market research, analysis, product development, more analysis, forecasting and planning, production, market introduction, and accelerated sales growth. This process cannot happen of its own volition, like spontaneous combustion; it must be made to happen.

Profitable new-product development is a logical, straight-forward procedure whereby ideas are encouraged, analyzed, and sifted. The best are developed into useful and marketable products, carefully and correctly introduced to the potential customers, and then sold in sufficient quantity to make the whole process worthwhile. All it really takes is a rational approach, a certain step-by-step methodology—and one good hard-working man to spearhead it.

EMPHASIZE THE P&L, NOT THE R&D

Before getting to the nitty gritty, some misconceptions must be laid to rest. The most common are:

1. A good new-product manager is an "idea" man.
2. The biggest task in new-product development is finding a "good idea."
3. New-product development is the natural output of R&D.
4. The best man to spearhead a new-product idea is its loudest champion—he thought it up and is best qualified to push it through.
5. The obvious choice is the sales manager/product manager for the company/section/division involved.

All nonsense—and the raw material of the adverse 19:1 odds. Profitable new-product development does not come from "doin' what comes natchurly." Let us examine these popular "hang ups" one by one.

1. *The "idea-man" myth.* First of all, a new product manager must be a very hard-headed, realistic business man. Not just a tried-and-true employee—a business man. An accomplished jack-of-all trades, equally conversant with marketing, sales, market research, production, production methods, and product design. He must be a manager and a salesman, able to win friends and influence people. He need not be an "idea man." Very few so-called "idea men" are capable of being new-product managers—and a good manager will find more marketable ideas than a dozen "idea men."
2. *Finding ideas.* This is the easiest part of all. Intelligent men in your company have discussed, ignored, and forgotten more ideas than you can evaluate in a life time. Do not worry about finding ideas. Once the new-product function is operational—indeed, long before—the ideas will find you.
3. *Research and development.* A nicely turned phrase, but usually a misleading

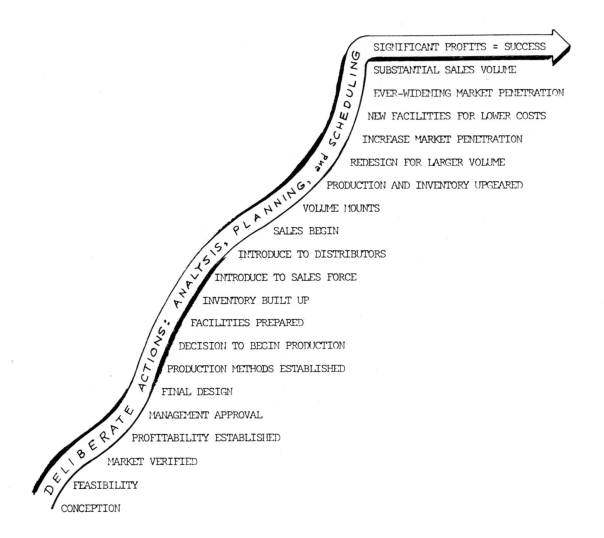

SIGNIFICANT PROFITS = SUCCESS

SUBSTANTIAL SALES VOLUME

EVER-WIDENING MARKET PENETRATION

NEW FACILITIES FOR LOWER COSTS

INCREASE MARKET PENETRATION

REDESIGN FOR LARGER VOLUME

PRODUCTION AND INVENTORY UPGEARED

VOLUME MOUNTS

SALES BEGIN

INTRODUCE TO DISTRIBUTORS

INTRODUCE TO SALES FORCE

INVENTORY BUILT UP

FACILITIES PREPARED

DECISION TO BEGIN PRODUCTION

PRODUCTION METHODS ESTABLISHED

FINAL DESIGN

MANAGEMENT APPROVAL

PROFITABILITY ESTABLISHED

MARKET VERIFIED

FEASIBILITY

CONCEPTION

ANALYSIS, PLANNING, and SCHEDULING

DELIBERATE ACTIONS:

Figure 1-2

The path of new-product development, from idea conception to significant profit and market penetration, is a long one. Careful planning is vital, if for no other reason than to see that no step is bypassed. The man who manages new-product development (regardless of his actual title) must keep the project moving, coordinating the activity of many departments. But notice—his job does not end when the product is introduced to the market. When the new product development is "completed" by most standards is actually when the most vital portion begins. A profitable new product is the end result of deliberate process, much of which occurs in the marketplace.

one; like "marketing" (what does that mean?). There are 450,000 words in an unabridged dictionary. A well-educated businessman might enjoy a working vocabulary of 15,000 or so. In all this profusion, it is unfortunate that "development" gets involved so often. R&D is a very serious function of many companies and, except when involved in projects for the federal government, is often productive of new ideas which are, or could be, marketed successfully. But this is merely raw material for new-product development. New-product development is, in essence, an inward extension of marketing; a digging within the company to find, develop, and offer for sale a product which is the fulfillment to a marketing opportunity. R&D is usually a search for the sake of searching. When well managed, its activities are guided along paths calculated to produce inventions which have market possibilities. But that is not new-product development—the two mingle, but do not become one—ever.

4. *The champion is the best man.* The best man to spearhead new-product development is NOT the champion of an idea. If anything will kill your chances of profitable new-product development, it is to have the new-product manager become the proud father of pet projects. Most of the thousands of new-product failures are attributable to such emotional seat-of-the-pants thinking. Joe has an idea, so let him see what he can do with it. But, even when Joe knows that he has a flop, he cannot give it up—his pride, reputation, and fatherhood are at stake. So the pet project gradually fades away—and another failure is chalked up.

5. *The sales manager/product manager.* The sales manager is seldom the ideal man—he has other and vital work to do. The product manager (assuming the commonest application of this nebulous term) might be. But the man in charge of new-product development should do that, and nothing more. The reason is that product development is short term; it requires a man who can pour tremendous energy and concentration into a project—for a while. Once the problems are solved and the new product is moving satisfactorily, he can move to the next project. Neither the sales manager nor the product manager are psychologically suited to do this—their inclinations, abilities, and interests must be long term. Further, both must devote their time and energy to those products which support the firm's volume and profits—they do not have time to mother a new product. So while new-product development may be a part-time sales or marketing department operation in many smaller firms, this is unlikely to be either satisfactory or profitable.

New-product development must be a profit-making operation. If it makes a profit, it succeeds. When it does not make a profit, it fails. It will do the former when it is properly managed. It will do the latter when it is not managed well. And by management, we mean careful market research to see what can be sold, analysis to see if profits can be realized, development of a suitable product to sell, and then deliberate forced sales growth to make certain that the plans and forecasts are consummated.

The purpose of new-product development is to make money. Its final assessment is the firm's P&L statement.

Chapter 2
The New-Product Program

> ...how to set up and manage a corporate program for successful new-product development. Nothing so far-reaching can be operated haphazardly. The success of the program will depend largely upon how well it is organized and grafted to the corporate structure. Here is how—and why—to make new-product development the sole responsibility of a specific task group.

LET'S SEE HOW IT'S DONE

In 1963 a highly regarded firm in the electronic-instrumentation field detected a market opportunity. An aggressive firm with "modern management," they went to an outside R&D firm and had them develop, at great expense, a sophisticated instrument utilizing technology at the outer limits of the state of the art. A few units were sold for some $6,000 apiece. Scenting victory, much more was spent (again with outside firms) in trying to develop a worthwhile sales brochure. Naturally, since the prospects were sophisticated engineers, the brochure had to be written at their level. This was finally abandoned because no two people agreed how the instrument worked, or what it did, or even what it was for.

Sales continued slowly, always to far-out labs who spent government money so were not too critical. But then it was discovered that the instrument did not function with the predicted accuracy, so all units sold were recalled for correction. A second outside engineering firm was retained to do this. The instruments were rebuilt and returned, and a number of additional ones were sold. Having abandoned the idea of a thorough, descriptive brochure, a quickie flyer was printed, containing vague charts and graphs and sketchy specifications. Unfortunately, the instrument filled a genuine marketing need and many more were sold before growing service problems forced acceptance of the fact that the instruments were unreliable. So, for a second time, all instruments were recalled. Because of their unhappy experience with outside engineering, the firm hired a genius to do the job right. He disagreed violently with the electronic techniques involved and started to redevelop the entire thing from scratch. They fired him, patched up the black boxes with more reliable components, and sent them back.

A year or so later a major supplier developed a product (as an accessory to one of the firm's existing instruments!) which would do everything that it was hoped the black boxes could do. Amid much fanfare this new instrument was introduced at a substantially reduced price. The new instrument was much more reliable than the old one and the unhappy owners of the old were forced to discard it and buy the new one. Sales surged ahead, but as might be expected in such a comedy of errors, the new instrument required manufacturing facilities already overloaded by popular, more profitable, and better established products. So naturally, delivery of the new instrument worsened rapidly, then become impossible. As of last acquaintance with the perils of this Pauline, all sales pressure had been withdrawn and it was hoped that customers for the new instrument would quietly go away.

This is typical new-product development in a "modern" firm. It is not exaggerated; worse yet, it is not even unusual. Going to market prematurely with an untried product, and an on-again off-again sales effort, are all too common. You would think that a company which had gone through this kind of mess would be slow about additional new-product adventures. But no, once-burned never seems to be twice-warned in new products.

The sample is typical of the new-product development procedure. There is ample room for improvement.

THE NAME OF THE GAME IS MONEY

No point in beating the obvious to death; it is self-evident that a profitable new product contributes to a company's financial well-being—and that an unsuccessful new product represents a dead loss. A loss because money was invested in it and no return was realized; a loss because that money invested elsewhere or handled differently might have produced a profit. Intelligent money management cannot permit investments in new-product development—not when the odds are 19:1 against success.

Twenty years ago, accounting was primarily an historical function. But today's treasurer looks at his company's financial health from a vastly different standpoint than did his predecessors. Today, the treasurer may be the one man in the company who could tell the president about the appalling loss from unsuccessful or breakeven new products, and the potential profits had those products been properly managed. Why is this not done? Or are new-product development costs so buried or disguised that no one knows what a new-product flop costs? Could this be the real reason why new-product development is so often conducted under the table?

Unfortunately, the treasurer, not being omniscient, can ask questions but must draw his conclusions from what he is told. Part of being an accountant, and so deeply entrenched in every financial man's thinking that he no longer questions it, is the fact that financial figures balance—they are self-proving. Too often financial people forget that theirs is probably the only area in a firm where this happens—and completely underestimate the amount to which so-called facts reported by other departments are nothing more than pure guesses. So the financial man builds his solid-appearing conclusions upon those reports which agree with his neat columns of figures.

For instance, a consultant found a product which a manufacturer had invented and introduced 20 years ago. But the product had attracted so much competition through the years that the firm currently enjoyed only 17% of the market! In a conversation with the treasurer of the company, that executive stated that the reason the company had been forced out of the market was because competitors were able to undersell it. Yet when salesmen were interviewed, they said the primary problem was slow delivery and too little inventory.

The treasurer knew his sales, cost, and profit figures and saw his competitors' price lists, so his conclusion is easy to understand. But the salesmen were in touch with customers, and convinced of their own viewpoint. Are executives like the blind men who examined the elephant, each one knowing only a different portion? Who is right—or are none of them?

Look at the problem: How is it possible for a company to invent and develop a product, accumulate 20 years of experience in manufacture and sales, and still have 83% of the total market snatched away by Johnny-come-latelys? Even the existence of such a fact should cause an immediate study to find out why. In this particular company, it took the consultant less than one day to find both problem and cause—the company set up production procedures for making the product 20 years ago—and had not changed them since. Of course, their costs were too high. And of course, their deliveries were too slow.

Why did the firm not correct the situation? Because sales volume did not permit the investment. And why was sales volume so low? Because costs were too high and deliveries were too slow. Et cetera, ad infinitum et nauseum.

No financial man should ever permit himself to complacently view such a situation in his firm. The dirty linen may not show up on the president's desk, but it most assuredly shows up in cost accounting, product/profit studies, and on the balance sheet. And any new-product manager should spot and investigate such a sleeping dog.

In this example, the firm pushed sales up until the shop was loaded and a comfortable backlog existed, then kept sales at that level—for 20 years! Apparently the firm actually did not realize that the market which they originally dominated had grown to some six times its original volume. This is not good new-product management—their loss of penetration is costing them $18 million in sales volume annually!

A properly managed new-product development program can make an absolutely night-and-day difference in the financial well-being and stability of any company. The profits should completely cancel the most cynical of ho-hum comments such as, "The founder has made so much money he doesn't care anymore" (he doesn't?), or "The company will probably be sold anyway" (then why not make it as valuable as possible?), or "If the president didn't like it that way he would change it" (has anyone showed him the problem—and a solution?).

IT ALL STARTS AT THE TOP

New-product development cuts across all departments in the company. It represents an established firm giving birth to a series of new ones. These new ones differ from a completely independent entity only in technicalities—the manager of the new-product operation is not in fact an entrepreneur; he is not in a position to initiate or to approve his own efforts. The impetus and the approval comes from the head of the parent—the president.

Successful and significant new-product development cannot exist in a company where the president and the board are not interested. And it has to be more than mere polite acquiescence. It must be a want—a recognized need—a living part of the president's concept of how his business should be run, and the reasons why it should be run that way.

From one viewpoint, it can be said that a president's job is two-fold: (1) to manage his company so as to maximize profits from yesterday's new products and (2) to manage so as to assure the success of tomorrow's new products. Very few presidents see their positions and duties in this light. Yet if you review the history of almost any firm you will see that the company *started* with a new product. Furthermore, as shown in Figures 2-1A and 2-1B its position today is the inevitable result of how well that first new product—and successive ones—were developed and managed. Its future depends largely—in many cases, entirely —on how carefully and successfully it is developing new products today, so that tomorrow it will have something to manage.

A corporation president is either dedicated to management and preservation of the status quo, and has placed (or developed) like-minded individuals in the managerial positions—or he is dedicated to constant progress of the company into newer areas and into wider markets and has brought this type of people around him. No company can go both ways.

The new-product manager can judge his president and what the president will actually do—as opposed to what he says he may do—by getting acquainted with the executive vice president and the men who head the areas of manufacturing, sales, and finance. If these four men are all of the same caliber (as is usually the case), then knowing them is usually equivalent to knowing the president. In your organization, if these people are all old soldiers dedicated to preserving the memory of their earlier campaigns—quit. If these four men are action-minded individuals willing to accept responsibility (of itself an extremely useful indicator), and who are pushing the company into an ever increasing share of its present market and perhaps into completely new markets—then they will reflect the president's intentions. Nothing as far reaching in scope as new-product development can come up from the bottom. The desire, the objectives, and the criteria must all start at the president's desk.

The only conceivable exception to the like-president, like-VP rule is the new president of an old firm, or that rare occasion where a president has accumulated a status-quo corporation around him but then wishes that he had not. In this case, the president (if not primarily concerned with his own retirement or with selling his firm and its problems), might conceive the desire to commence a new-product campaign. He could merely be waiting for the arrival of the right man. The president would know

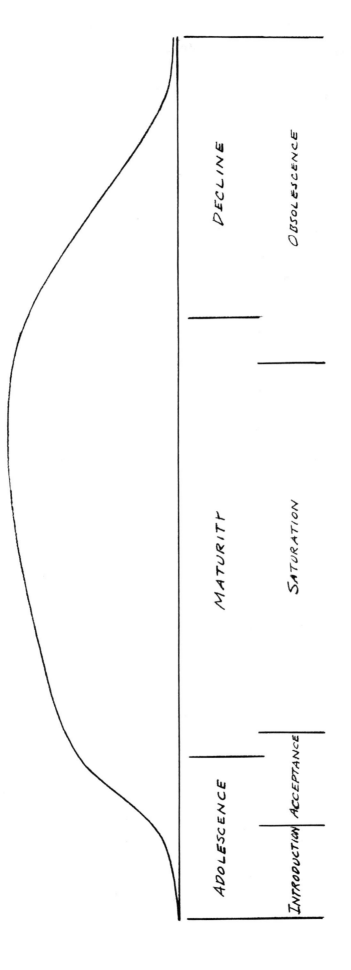

ADOLESCENCE

INTRODUCTION | ACCEPTANCE

MATURITY

SATURATION

DECLINE

OBSOLESCENCE

Figure 2-1A

The marketing life of a specific product always follows the same course: a tentative beginning, then rapid growth during an adolescent period until it reaches some level of saturation. Growth then levels off and becomes more parallel with the economic climate of the times until a peak is finally reached—full marketing maturity. This peak may be a long plateau, but eventually the product becomes subject to the pressure of competing newer ideas and decline begins. In some cases (such as kerosene lamps) the product is resurrected to begin a new life cycle.

With consumer products, this cycle can be very short—only a season for a fad product or even less for one jumped on by the government. But for industrial products which survive their introduction, the life cycle is usually quite long—perhaps many decades.

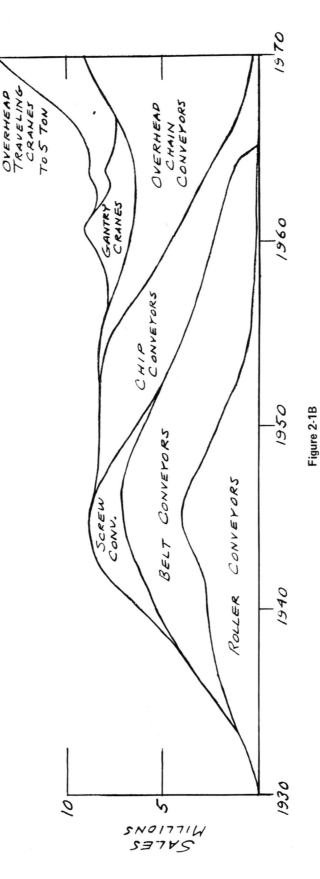

Figure 2-1B

The history of any individual firm's activity with a given product is the same sort of curve as shown in Figure 2-1A, but the total life span is usually shorter. This is because a firm is a living thing, twisting and turning in the market place as it searches out profitable routes, abandoning products which have become unprofitable or are found to be unattractive.

In the hypothetical firm shown, during a 40-year period its first, second, and fourth products were phased out, after a profitable life span. Belt conveyors were cut off abruptly to avoid low-volume losses, while roller conveyors and chip conveyors (where profit was not so volume-sensitive) have been allowed to decline naturally. Screw conveyors and gantry cranes were quickly dropped. Overhead conveyors now carry the firm, with cranes becoming increasingly important. Notice the shift within the product mix, with simple (low dollars per unit) items gradually supplanted by more sophisticated products, involving systems sales, higher engineering content, and more advanced production facilities.

that his status-quo management echelons contained no suitable men—there may have been at one time, but the years would have browbeaten the ability out of them. Under the circumstances, both the president and the "right" man are fortunate to meet—*provided* the president has the courage to stand behind his new-product man during the inevitable bloody clashes which will occur. A pot which has not been stirred in years will strongly resist the spoon.

THE MASTER OF CEREMONIES

The new-product manager's job is not a flunky position, to be held by someone's nephew or old college chum—nor is it a safe haven for an ineffective but loyal employee until he retires. It is one of the most important jobs in the firm—and certainly one of the most difficult.

It is so important because the company's entire future may well depend upon the success of its new-product ventures. A steady succession of properly developed new products assures future growth and profits. No firm is likely to go downhill if most of its new products are successful, a few are extremely so, and none are complete flops. But a company with a history of unsuccessful new-product ventures—or worse, one which has not even made the attempt—is dying on the vine. An upswing in the aggressiveness of competitors, a shift in technology, or introduction of a new idea by someone else could easily be the death knell of the firm.

So the new-product manager will have a profound effect upon his company's future. As he succeeds, so does his company. If he fails, or is not permitted to succeed, or gets hopelessly lost in internal politics and becomes ineffectual, the company has lost its best opportunity of assuring tomorrow. No company can consider itself modern, aggressive, well managed—indeed, even safe—unless it has a functioning new-product development operation, and one which has a good track record. The man who manages this operation is a very important member of the corporate structure, one who should be carefully selected and then assisted in every possible way to assure his successes.

And that assistance will be necessary, for the new-product manager's job is one of the most difficult, (and often frustrating) of any within the corporation. This is so because his is a staff, rather than a line position. But unlike most staff operations, which tend to be advisory or investigatory, the new-product manager and his group must produce. And this involves working with the entire spectrum of the firm: R&D, engineering, production, sales, advertising, financial, purchasing, and top-management people. He cannot follow the normal vertical chain of command since he needs to move horizontally, working with every box on the organization chart.

And therein lies the rub—the new-product manager's responsibility is enormous, but his authority is virtually nil, limited to his own staff. Practically everything that he must accomplish will actually be done by people who do not work for him; who do not accept orders from him; who probably will not understand the importance of assisting him; and who will do his work if and when they "have time" from their regular duties. So the new-product manager is in the unenviable position of being charged with great responsibilities yet utterly without the authority to see that the bulk of his work gets done.

In principle, the new-product manager's job is a one-man band. In practice, he is a conductor. His applied psychology and salesmanship must be first rate, because he is working with volunteers—benefiting from the labors of individuals whom he can inspire, cajole, or seduce, but whom he cannot command.

To be sure, there is a bit of steel in his velvet glove: he can "tell on" those who are not nice to him. Having access to the top of the ladder, he can report lack of cooperation and in this way enforce his requests for assistance. But if he relies on aid from the top very often, the president will soon suspect that he picked the wrong man for the job—and with justification.

The new-product manager must be capable of performing his job—and to a very large degree, that job consists of getting cooperation from all those people in the organization who can help him when so inclined.

Of course, he can force cooperation when his wishes are supported by official edict from the president. But the difference between active assistance and enforced tolerance is dramatic. If he can win help, support, and cooperation, his job is possible and practical. But if he can get it only by wearing the president's last action AVO on a string around his neck, the job is, for all intents and purposes, completely impossible.

EVERYBODY GETS INTO THE ACT

Like no one else in the entire company, the new-product manager must be a successful and experienced jack-of-all-trades. *He must* understand the problems, know how to work with (and how to benefit from the experience of) machine operators, production foremen, research people, engineers, and all department heads, including the chief engineer, the plant superintendent, the vice president of manufacturing, purchasing agent, head of cost accounting, treasurer, advertising manager, the field salesmen, sales manager, president—and everyone in between. It tends to keep a man on his toes.

But the fact is that the new-product manager must work his magic through others. His greatest dangers come from within himself. Since his personal experience is most unlikely to have encompassed all the functions with which he must work, he is bound to be ignorant (and worse, unsympathetic) toward some. Secondly, his strong entrepreneurial instincts will cause him to believe that he can do most tasks faster and better than the next man. While he may be right, it is suicidal to indulge his feelings. If he develops the new product single-handedly, it will be resisted by precisely those people who must become interested in it and ultimately adopt it as their own—engineering, production, and sales. The new-product manager must, by working through others, see his projects brought to fruition and maturity as significant parts of the company's product line. When each reaches the desired maturity, it must be turned over for routine handling. And this will never happen if the idea has been developed independently and in spite of the departments who must ultimately work with it.

If not natural to him, the new-product manager must develop that slightly cynical attitude whereby he can (with minimum misgivings) plant his ideas in the minds of others, so that he can help them reap these ideas as their own. This may, in some cases, be his only way: to help the brilliant department head further his own idea, rather than try to fight men who may never have had an idea. The author certainly does not intend to reveal his own ignorance by practicing amateur psychology, but the scars from many new-product campaigns has taught what works versus what does not work.

Each new product moves through a dozen departments—each a potential friction area. So, the new-product manager must have a working knowledge of each of these departments—not only the people, but the work. While it is not expected that he become a broad-spectrum expert in every field, it is vital that he be well acquainted with them as they relate to new products. At every stage he has to be able to evaluate suggestions and plans proposed by the specialists involved. In many cases he will have to come up with his own plan and either sell it or plant it. Often he will have to boost department heads out of deeply rutted thought paths. By definition, a new product is something outside the normal routine of the company. There is a danger: if a new product drops into the routine of any of the departments through which it must move, it stands an excellent chance of being killed—or at least horribly delayed.

For an example, advertising. Envision a major capital-equipment maker, established around the turn of the century (likely to be a classic example of conservative business practices, particularly if still family held). Somebody within this firm comes up with a useful and potentially profitable new design. After research and engineering, it becomes a reality, obtains the president's blessing, and is ready to present to the customer. En route, the advertising manager gets involved. Unfortunately, the chances are 99 to 100 that the advertising manager's thinking is extremely conservative, a parody embodying his notions of the president; an attempt to outdo his boss. Since most of the products which he advertises have been manufactured for many years (and the president cannot correlate advertising and sales anyway), some senility and complacency at his level (and maybe higher up) are to be expected.

However, as shown in Figure 2-2, the introduction of a new product poses a completely different advertising problem than the routine ho-hum promotion of well-established products. It is possible that the advertising manager will recognize this and leap to the challenge. But not very likely. In this case, the new-product manager must know (or must very rapidly learn) how to introduce a new product via advertising.

He must insist upon an objective appraisal of magazine advertising, publicity, public relations, trade shows, direct mail, skywriting, or whatever else may occur to him as worth analysis, completely disregarding how the company now promotes its routine products and regardless of any prejudices concerning various promotion tools. He cannot accept a comment like, "We do not exhibit at trade shows because our competitors do not." This may be fine for the mundane day-to-day advertising of established products. But such thinking can be nothing but disastrous when enforced on a new product. After an objective appraisal of all alternative promotional methods, he must work with the advertising manager to produce the campaign most likely to get the desired results.

So the new-product manager must know advertising—and market research, design and engineering in his company's field, tool-and-die design, process engineering,

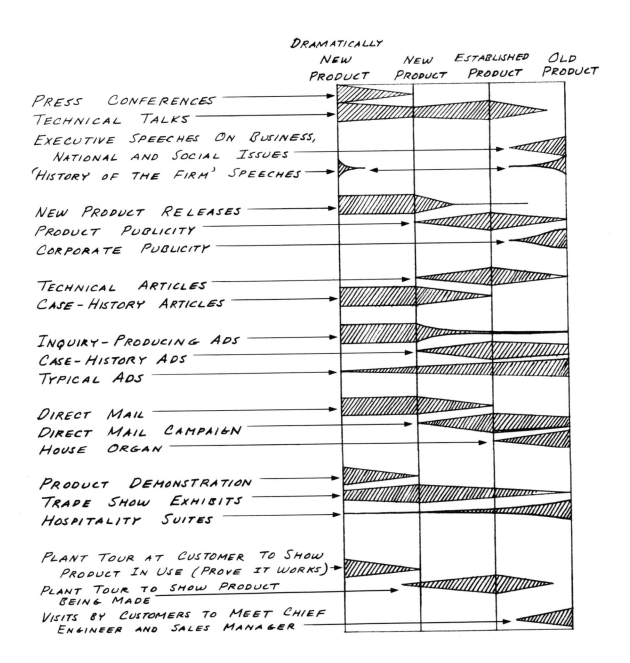

Figure 2-2

New products require and benefit from a different selection of promotion tools than those employed for well established products. If advertising and promotion are to be of value in developing new-product sales volume, the firm must set aside policies and practices that are not productive. Conversely, a wide-awake firm can hasten the growth of its new products by employing promotion tactics which may not occur to its competitors.

costing, investment analysis, inventory control, and a host of specialties. In no other way can he evaluate others' plans—or know when he is being conned.

Managing new-product development is not an easy job—but it is certainly an interesting and challenging one.

THE GOOD OLD DAYS

A formal new-product program rocks the boat. Appointing a new-product manager will, too. By the program's very existence it forces deliberate investigation, analysis, and decision making. It requires prior commitment by department heads, scheduling, and deadlines. *It requires thinking.* And it requires planning.

All too often these are unfamiliar and uncomfortable activities for a company. American management is an astonishingly successful phenomenon, but in spite of its successes, the plain fact is that most companies operate purely by the seat of their pants. Fantastically important decisions are made on the spur of the moment, following no real analysis, and with no weighing of alternatives. In precisely those areas where a company should study before it moves, too many companies jump wildly. In areas where speed is essential, too many companies procrastinate. This is because companies are made up of people and people behave in this manner. It's natural.

A formal new-product campaign requires someone to operate it, someone to be responsible. Informal, "like Topsy" new-product development is sort of cooperative. It takes place within the existing organization; nobody is responsible, nobody sticks his neck out very far. In these comfortable circumstances, a new product is developed in a procedure about like the following:

Over a period of two or three years a number of the company's salesmen urge the firm to start making a product because it fits into their experience area and customers ask for it. These suggestions are usually taken "under consideration." If the salesmen are persistent, somewhere along the line engineering or manufacturing finally decides whether or not they can make (want to bother with) the product. After enough salesmen have asked for the product, the sales manager pressures management into a yes-we-can or no-we-cannot decision. Sometime at lunch, sandwiched into a conversation about something else, or in a 30-second conversation over the office intercom, the sales manager tells the president, "Manufacturing says 'we can make it,' and our men tell us that there's a lot of customers who want to buy it from us."

The president says he will check with manufacturing. A few months later it is understood by a form of executive osmosis that the green light has been given. If a number of sizes are involved, the decision must be made whether to make a full line or an abbreviated line. The sales manager checks with the two or three salesmen who happen to be in the office one day and asks them what sizes their customers use. One of the salesmen knows nothing about it. One of them has been asking for the product recently, and the third salesman put in a strongly worded request two years ago. Forced to come up with fast answers without time to think or check their notes, the two salesmen rattle off some sizes. The sales manager retires to his den with a competitor's brochure, circles the sizes which his survey has revealed to be the most popular, and blocks out the size range.

A copy of the marked-up sheet goes to manufacturing as advance warning that the salesmen will go after orders immediately. Another copy goes to the advertising department with a note something like, "There is a tremendous market out there which we are going after. Work up a hard-sell brochure as fast as you can. The salesmen need it badly."

Within a week or so the first orders move in from the most active salesmen and distributors, the ones most likely to put the new product over the top. But of course, production is not ready yet, the inventory at best is spotty, no thinking has been done on quoting or other vital matters. So the key people who can push the product get burned with bad delivery and soon drop it. A year later the new product is active, bobbing along in the wake of its own birth defects. Perhaps some day it will make a profit. In any case, it's now part of the product line and can fend for itself.

And this is called new-product development.

Actually, this procedure has many advantages over doing the job formally. First, no one is rushed; years are available. Second, all decisions are made on the safe side. Third, sales costs are kept low by giving the salesmen permission to go after only the cream of the customers. Fourth, since the field and home office people know their business, no market research is needed. Fifth, the design is a Chinese copy of competitive offerings, which eliminates expensive research and engineering. Sixth, only long-established competitors are considered. This avoids copying any new and controversial designs which may well be better—but then, may not be. Seventh, investment is kept minimal, since investment in both inventories and production facilities is done cautiously, based upon sales obtained. This can be even better safeguarded by slow delivery, so there is always a backlog to protect material and in-process inventory investments.

These benefits alone are more than sufficient. Any company who can afford a 95% failure rate among its new products should most certainly stay with an informal program.

Ideas Worth Exploring--No. 1

RADIAL-ARM DRILL PRESS

Description: The machine incorporates a base, column, and an extendable head mounted on hinged arms. Similar to radial-arm type skin routers except that a conventional drilling head is used. A tapping head is an obvious alternate.

History: The machine shown was manufactured by The Foote-Burt Company of Cleveland, Ohio, from before World War II up through the early '60s, then was dropped as their business shifted into large special-purpose equipment. The firm has shown some reawakened interest lately. The design was based upon light-duty drill presses made well before the turn of the century.

Marketing Comments: Such a machine should be made in a number of sizes, ranging from extremely light hand-feed drill presses through the same capacity ranges now served by conventional column-and-arm radial drill presses. A radial-arm drill press of this design could be less expensive than a conventional radial drill press of the same capacity—not substantially more expensive than ordinary drill presses or drilling machines.

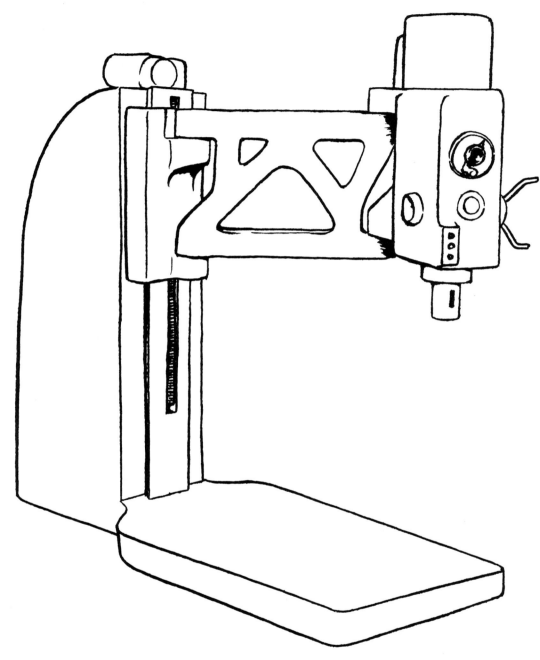

NOTE: This is one of a number of "Ideas Worth Exploring" presented in this book. The author *has not* done this exploring. If a patent is known, it is listed. No listing does *not* mean that the idea is unpatented, or that it can be legally used in any way. Most good ideas have been patented, at one time or another. Most patents have expired and many current ones could probably be contested if literature research turned up prior exposure, as would certainly be the case with many ideas, particularly in the older fields, such as mechanical. *Nevertheless,* none of the ideas given in this book are represented as being free of patents—and the author accepts no responsibility or liability from the use of any of these ideas.

Chapter 3
The New-Product Manager's Job

> . . .the new-product development group functions both at the staff and the operational level. The dual level imposes built-in problems—and the manager's most demanding task is to function gracefully at both levels. This chapter shows how it is done—and how the manager, from his own viewpoint, must assess the firm and his chances for success.

SETTING UP SHOP

There is no pattern to organization for new-product development. Most firms have none. Among those firms who have organized, there are a dozen systems employed. These vary somewhat with the industry involved, but mostly with the size of the firm and the personality of the president—specifically, his interest in new-product development and his habits concerning delegation. Not delegation of work—delegation of authority; whether authority is delegated because the president has developed competent management men, or whether he just does not want to be bothered.

In smaller firms (or large ones run in a small-firm paternalistic fashion), new product development is often handled personally by the president—nobody else in the place has any brains and he has to do it himself. Or the work may be delegated to his assistant or some other executive, who may devote all or part of his time to new products. This may be an excellent arrangement—often better than the committee systems too often found in large firms. If someone works full time on new-product development, his title will be new-product manager, product-planning manager, planning coordinator, etc. Any title seems acceptable as long as it has currently popular "action words": planning, coordination, development, new, future, etc. If a committee runs the show, then words like "action" and "profit" appear. "Liaison" is seldom found, probably because no one knows how to spell it, or because the French are still in a popularity slump. But it has a nice ring to it.

A problem enters when the new-product development function is a part-time venture. Usually the man involved finds it difficult to step far enough away from his primary function to be as objective as is necessary for product development. The sales manager/new-product manager looks at new products through his sales-department eyes—and so on. The risk is lessened if the man is in marketing or sales and is greater as his department gets farther from contact with the market. Engineers and R&D people have the least chance of success as new-product managers. If the man involved is not the head of his department, he probably will not have the access to top management which is vital for profitable long-term new product management. In most firms where new-product development is pushed down to the level of some department head's assistant—it does not exist.

When a firm uses a committee arrangement, some benefits accrue—to the members; not the firm. First, responsibility is spread too thinly to be burdensome. Second, everyone has an enjoyable opportunity to express opinions, usually without the necessity of doing any homework first. Third, committees operate under primitive sociological rules. Once the pecking order has been established, either by the president's displayed approval or simply by survival of the most vulgar, the meetings become more relaxed because everyone knows which man will win. Without implying that a committee is an ineffectual organism, the fact remains that most are merely resonant chambers for one man's voice. Dr. Lazo analyzed the types of new-product functions and found that (1) committees are involved in the majority, (2) 75% of firms responding to surveys were unhappy with their new-product organization, and (3) marketing men directed new-product development in less than 10% of the firms. This keeps the odds at 19:1.

The ideal structure for the new-product development function involves two leading characters, the president (or executive VP) and the new-product manager. (See Figure 3-1.) Often a committee, preferably chairmanned by the VP marketing, and consisting of heads of R&D, engineering, production, finance, sales, and/or other departments, fits between the lead characters. This may be a good thing. Usually it is not. The new-product manager should not be presenting plans to these men for approval—they should have been helping him develop the plans to start with. Their thinking should help mold the new product, not be a gauntlet for it to run.

The structure must be made to fit the process, not the other way around. A new-product idea follows a simple, direct route:

1. Conception and preliminary evaluation
2. Review to see if the *development* expense looks like a good investment
3. Design development of product, tooling, and obtain detailed data on markets, competition, costs, etc.
4. Analysis of the fruit of the development, as supported by mature marketing and financing data and forecasts
5. Exploitation—starting production, introducing product to the market; the kick off

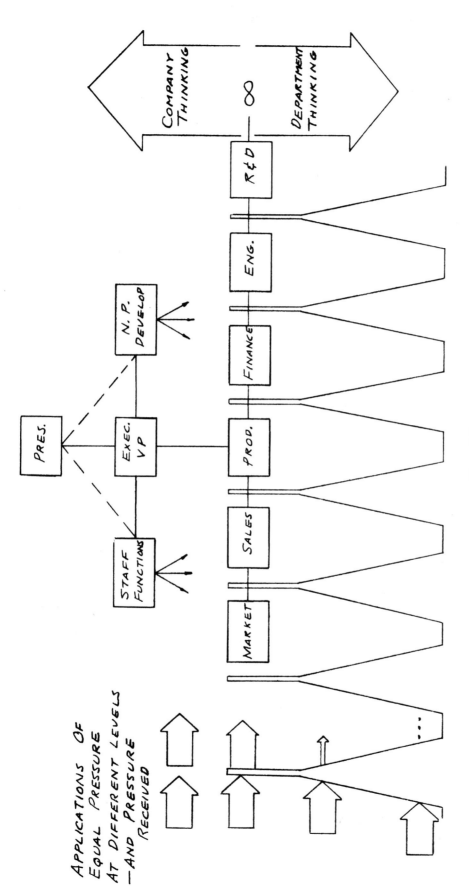

Figure 3-1

The new-product manager must operate near the upper reaches of the management structure because his duties require that he move horizontally within the firm. If he is dropped into one of the departmental structures, his mobility is sharply reduced. And if he is low in the echelon of any single department, his mobility is virtually nonexistent. Notice that like most solid structures, the walls between departments are thickest at the bottom.

New-product development, to be successful, must be a staff function.

6. Follow through, feedback, correction, and intensive continuing sales effort to build product to market maturity

The first step is the only one which the new-product manager can do alone. For all the other steps, the new product manager merely coordinates and MC's the work of other departments. Perhaps a committee can do this, but it can be done faster and more efficiently by a good manager. Steps 2 and 4 are decision making. Here a committee has logical purpose. They can explore a presentation in detail and report their findings to the president for final approval.

Thus, the most efficient arrangement for profitable new-product development emerges:

A new-product manager, whose duties include finding product and marketing opportunities, makes a preliminary evaluation and prepares a proposal for review and approval. If approved, he puts his proposal into effect. This involves nursemaiding, scheduling, followup, and coordination as the project moves through many departments. Meanwhile, he, his staff, or people in other departments are finalizing data. When all is ready, the product exists as a joint venture by all concerned. He presents the final data and projections for review and approval. If approved, the product goes into production and the new-product manager shifts his attention to assisting sales as volume is pushed to the projected levels.

A new-product review committee should confine itself to review of the basic idea, extending the benefit of their experience, and making suggestions. But as shown in Figure 3-2, decision should rest only with the president, executive VP, or VP marketing—the only three men actually qualified to make a new-product decision.

The same committee (or one with a slightly different membership) should *assist* the new-product manager in presenting the fully developed and analyzed product to the president for the final decision about whether or not to go into production. The committee members will have contributed heavily to the product; they are no longer in a position to evaluate it.

The final decision maker can only be the president, executive VP, or head of the division involved. When such vital decisions are delegated, the entire venture is suspect. Unless, of course, the president is only titular head and somebody else holds the reins.

Certain attributes are desirable in a new-product manager—not that a successful manager must possess them all, but a wise man knows his shortcomings so that they do not become limitations. The manager must be an entrepreneur, a self starter, ambitious, a problem solver/challenge accepter, a man who does not necessarily accept what he is told—who has to find out. He must know the industry in which his firm operates (and preferably several others, too) and must have a well-developed intuitive sense for what is marketable. He must have an analytical bent and be able to think along objective, logical routes (often a difficult task). But above all, he must be able to woo and win the active support of others. He is a conductor, not first violinist. He must sell ideas, sell new-product development as a vital function, obtain active assistance, get others to work to schedules and deadlines, ease political tangles, plant ideas, and evaluate suggestions—and still not get so involved in a specific project that he is unable to accept a "kill it" decision from his boss.

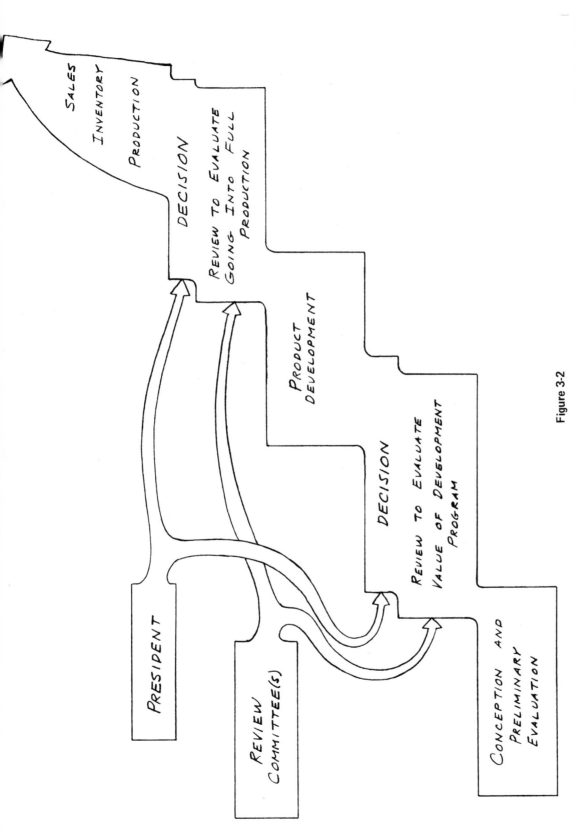

Figure 3-2

New-product development requires a manager—one man who will carry the ball. It cannot be done by a committee nor is joint (herd) effort likely to be successful. The committee is most useful as a review board—not to make decisions, but to be certain that the project is ready for a decision by top management.

One other thing. The new-product manager must not be myopic—very often an idea leads ultimately not to internal development, but to purchase of an existing maker of the product. So the new-product manager must develop the ability to look at potential competitors and visualize them as part of the firm. In an acquisition-minded company, he may be in a unique position to help evaluate potential buys.

And finally, the successful new-product manager has probably had broad experience—many firms and many positions. A reformed job-skipper is more likely to succeed than a man who has risen through the ranks of one firm. If the manager's interests and experience are narrow, he is likely to limit new products to a specific market or product type, which is generally not desirable.

The president, the firm, and the manager are ready to go. What comes first? More work for the president: he must define the corporate marketing goals. Since the new-product manager's job is to help achieve them, they have to be established. They should include:

1. Whether to confine new products to the presently served markets or to spread out.
2. Whether new products should be capable of manufacture with existing facilities and materials familiar to engineering and production.
3. Whether to stay with products which fit present distribution channels—and the present sales force.
4. Whether to stay with products within the experience and capabilities of the present engineering, production, and service staffs.
5. Whether or not to assign priority to products which can be sold by present distributors and salesmen to present customers.
6. Potential sales volume minimum, either for total product by all makers or for the firm alone. This may be stated as minimum percentage of penetration.
7. State clearly any specific taboos: i.e., nothing electronic, etc.
8. If the president has personal prejudices or preferences, he should state them. Don't be coy—the new product manager will learn them eventually and a lot of wasted effort can be avoided if the cards are on the table.
9. Rough performance criteria, i.e., must break even in X months, pay off capital investment in X years, achieve 10% market penetration in X months, etc. Careful—these must be guides, not rules.

These goals and limits must be thought out very carefully. If not practical and usable, they have no value. But they cannot be too confining—a company cannot concentrate on greater and greater depth in an extremely narrow market and have new-product development be meaningful. Conversely, it is ridiculous to say "anything within material handling" and yet have the president retain strong but unstated prejudices for or against certain areas.

THE SORCERER'S APPRENTICES

Work actually done by the new-product development group consists primarily of information gathering (market data, competitor intelligence, state-of-the-art, tentative costing, etc.), planning and scheduling (including preparation of flow sheets, time-tables, etc.), liaison work with other departments, forecasting and preparation of proposals and presentations, and field work with the sales department (either in selling or research activity). In a small operation, the new-product manager will do this work himself—for awhile. Then he will need help.

The most likely first need is for a numbers man with a feel for marketing, since information gathering and evaluation is both vital and time consuming. Such men, particularly those young enough to be attracted by the pay available, are hard to find. The best place is among accountant types: shop clerks, timekeepers, men in payroll departments, etc. They can be taught a feel for marketing, but an affinity for numbers is natural to some men and that is the type needed. A marketing graduate is too likely to be hung up on visions of glamour. He is tempted to add "English" to the figures, rush the work, and push onward to advertising, sales, and other "significant" phases.

The second man needed, however, *is* the marketing type, able to do field research, hold product introductions, work with salesmen and distributors, etc. Finding a good one may pose problems, but the colleges are shelling out marketing types so the supply is plentiful. To be of maximum value, he will need a carefully planned experience-gaining program. The best way is to put down on paper all the attributes of the ideal man. Then list the abilities of the man hired and plan a program to provide him with the missing experience. This may involve loaning him to other departments for indoctrination—engineering, production, R&D. If some way can be found to build some actual shop experience, it will greatly enhance the young man's value.

Ultimately help will be needed in the time-consuming but sensitive areas of coordination—working with the departments through which each project must move. Here the needs are different—a thorough familiarity with the makeup of the departments involved is vital and an easy, first-name familiarity with the department heads is often useful. Pick your personalities carefully. Stay away from a man who antagonizes with excessive familiarity, and from the one whose new duties will go to his head. Nonetheless, the touchy liaison duties are usually best handled by men promoted from within.

You will notice that idea generators have not been suggested. They will not be, because they are not welcome. If they belong anywhere, it is in the R&D lab, not in new-product *development*. The idea is merely the seed. All else is work. Idea men tend to be too unrealistic, and often cling tenaciously to an idea, defending it against all comers. What is needed are people who can remain objective until a plan is approved, grab the ball and run with it if management flashes the green light, yet drop it without a quiver if they get the red light.

Since new-product development covers a lot of territory, the individuals within the group will have widely varying backgrounds and widely divergent specialities. Yet they must be able to work together; many men but one team. No special climate is required other than that which a good manager can provide—esprit de corps, interest, a sense of progress and accomplishment, a feeling of being "inside"—party to important decisions—a unity of purpose, and pride. He must establish and maintain the best of rapport within the group, since it is in the business of maintaining rapport outside the group. Misfits and politicians must be weeded out as quickly as they are identified.

Special incentives are not needed, although of course, salaries must be on a par with other men of like capabilities in the company. The job is interesting, challenging, and satisfying—much more so than most line functions which tend to become cluttered with routine operations. New-product development is one part of the company where management by exception does not work. Therefore, the accomplishments of the individual are easily noted and should be recognized. The men will be useful in direct ratio to their certainty that they are going in the right direction. This can only come about by the manager's openness, his leadership, and pats on the back for a good job well done.

GETTING THE WORK DONE

The new-product manager and his group will seldom encounter problems in handling work done within the department—market research, data analysis, competitor intelligence, making reports and presentations, and so on. The rub comes when the group works with the rest of the firm. The objective is simple—to get new-product projects through the company. The methods employed, however, must be adapted for each project and for each man involved. The new-product people must become chameleons—adjusting their coloration to suit the personality of each department head.

Contacts with each department occur at four distinct levels: informal opinion gathering, discussion and appraisal of specific ideas, obtaining agreement on products to propose and confirmation of estimates, then work on approved new-product projects.

The first contact—informal opinion gathering—is a two-way street, getting thoughts on an idea and thoughts for an idea. Of course, this goes on constantly—you do not make appointments to accept ideas. Most talks about ideas occur with people from R&D, engineering, production, methods, finance, and sales. Ideas and useful comments are most likely to originate in these areas. Also, these men are most likely to have valid objections or spot defects in an idea.

Tentative new-product ideas could be discussed in a committee—but one antagonistic member can kill an idea. If preliminary discussions are private, then negative reactions are isolated while the new-product group explores the validity of their objections.

The talks may be made by the new-product manager himself or may be delegated. Thoughtful, honest, conscientious opinions are wanted. This often requires personal acquaintance with each department head. The liaison man involved should know his man, know whether to talk to him in the forenoon or afternoon, at his desk or in the coffee shop, at lunch or over a beer in the evening. The man must be in a comfortable, relaxed, unhurried, and unaggravated mood—free to think about something new.

If the new-product group decides to carry the idea through the proposal stage, the next round of meetings is more specific, concerned with design features, cost estimates, lead times, finding and pinning down potential problems.

With men who have good memories, the meetings can be private; but if a man has a slippery memory, take another department head along. These meetings provide the raw material for the proposal. A man cannot be permitted to say one thing at the pre-proposal stage and then refute his estimate after the proposal is assembled.

The biggest problem, of course, is with the department head who was against the idea to start with. With him, selling is needed—show him that other department heads are in favor of the idea and that the present step is only a development proposal. If he will become specific about the problems foreseen, perhaps they can be solved, or at least avenues of exploration can be found. Objections, valid or not, cannot be ignored. If they are run over rough shod, they will become haunts in conversations, excuses for procrastination, and openings for I-told-you-so's. And when top management discovers that valid *sounding* objections were willfully ignored, the entire proposal becomes suspect. A great deal of personal salesmanship is involved in working with recalcitrant department heads. Expect it—you'll need it.

The third contact comes after the new-product group has hammered out the rough draft of the proposal, based largely upon the information and estimates provided by the department heads. In meetings of two or three at a time (not individually), go over the rough draft in detail. The reason for meeting in small groups is to provide an audience/witnesses. Each man is performing before his peers—he is on his honor and now cannot deny earlier comments and estimates. The entire idea cannot be sandbagged by one man unless he has honest, unanticipated objections.

By having each head review the proposal at this stage, any awkward areas are smoothed out long before management sees the proposal. By the time it is polished and presented to management, all concerned know that it represents an objective, unified consensus of the opinions and estimates of all. This practically eliminates the possibility of any department head shooting down the project.

An integral part of every new-product proposal is the project plan, all worked out in advance. Therefore, if top management approves the program, the stage is already set for starting the work. Each department head knows what he is going to do, how long it will take him, and what he estimated it would cost. Each department head commences his portion of the work, knowing what the other departments are doing, and that he is performing to an audience. In this way, the work gets done rapidly and efficiently. Nobody can hide a dragging foot.

USING NONEXISTENT AUTHORITY

By setting up the new-product development group, the president said to the rest of the company, "Play ball." In time, when the new-product manager and his group have worked with the different department heads on a project or two, they will become welded into a unified group, all supporting the company's new-product activities. Since the proposals represent the *joint* thinking of all concerned, cooperation is virtually automatic—virtually, not necessarily. But when the proposal is approved by the president, the department heads are put on notice that their joint proposal has been accepted; they are given the green light to proceed. But more: they are ordered to do so. Therefore, the new-product manager will seldom encounter absolute refusals in coaxing the development project through the company.

However, there are many ways of avoiding work. Each department head is an individual; each will react quite differently at this stage, since commencing the work is much different than merely talking about it. The biggest danger is delay. Using the press of routine work as an excuse, the project slows, stumbles, and stops. And each department head will probably be guilty to a greater or lesser degree. Yet each has said what he can do, how long it will take, what it will cost, and the others have accepted his word for it. Be certain that each realizes that he is on stage: subject the entire project to the white glare of internal publicity. Every second week make up a status report, comparing the accomplishments with the projections (design, data collection, costs, time), and make certain that everybody involved in the company is on the list. When one department holds up the show, let everybody in the company know. Thus the laggard department invites criticism from both its fellows and from the president, yet the new-product manager cannot be accused of going upstairs to bring pressure to bear.

In rare cases, a department head will actively support all kinds of programs, forecasts and scheduling—but never do his share, finding new reasons why it won't work, finding higher priority tasks, or just do the work so slowly that it amounts to no progress at all.

If the president is unwilling or unable to move such stone statues, the new-product manager will have to devise ways of working around the roadblock. This can take many forms, all of them risky, and careful thought should be given before playing this game. But it can be done. Work can be farmed outside the firm. Often R&D or engineering can be used to bypass the other; tool design could be done between engineering and production; and so on. Usually, being bypassed once is enough—there is too much attention, too much exposure and criticism involved. Next time around, the bypassed department head will probably hasten to fall in line.

But beware—this is playing with fire. The new-product manager needs to get the support of those department heads who are involved. If this cannot be done, the entire program is in jeopardy.

WATCHING OUT FOR TENDER TOES

Anything outside the historical routine of the firm will be resented. Anything new is resented. And new-product development, being both non-routine *and* new, will cause resentment where it hurts most—among the department heads who must actually work in the development. This is a personality problem and can only be solved by the new-product manager's personal salesmanship. A recalcitrant department head should be approached both frontally and circuitously: frontally to overcome his *stated* opinions, and via the back door to solve or neutralize his real hangup.

A frontal approach must *not* be an attack—that solidifies the obstruction. Instead, play the game; be helpful. The most effective confessor approach depends upon the form of the alleged problem:

"Short handed." Find out what has changed in the man's department since the proposal was agreed upon; perhaps the project can be simplified, or handled by other departments, or a man borrowed, or the work farmed out.

"Another high-priority project." Who assigned the priority? This could be legitimate, but probably is not. Projects just do not pop out of nowhere—each department head knows what he can expect in terms of workload. New-product development must be worked in, the same as other tasks.

"Unexpected technical problems (we tried it and it doesn't work)." Again, this could be legitimate. But the name of the game is *development.* Snags are expected. It should be assumed that alternate approaches or solutions will need to be discovered, tried out, and the best selected. It is the new-product manager's job to see that potential difficulties are anticipated in the original proposal so that nobody goes into a funk when they occur.

But most of this is just smokescreen. When a man slows the project it is because he feels threatened or hurt. His sense of security, of self-importance, has been endangered. This can be for many reasons—he feels inferior to those about him, the development may uncover areas of ignorance or inability and he fears exposure and criticism, he is a one-man band and antagonistic to cooperative ventures—anything, any foible of the human psyche, any quirk caused by anything in his history since childhood.

But the new-product manager must not become an amateur psychologist. If he is already so inclined, such inclinations should be saved for cocktail parties. A much safer and surer route is to search out a middleman. If a department head balks at carrying out his part of the development, find men who are his friends, men whom he respects, men for whom he will unbend. Sell them on the new-product function, point out that it has the president's blessing, and that this man is inviting the criticism of too many people by sandbagging the project. In this way, most men can be wooed—just find the right John Alden.

If the new-product manager is a relative newcomer, the middleman may be most useful by getting the manager and the laggard department head together some night for a few drinks. Sometimes this works wonders. Sometimes all fails. Then it is a problem for the boss.

GETTING ALONG WITH THE BOSS

This is applied marketing—personal marketing. Know what the president wants done, then do it.

The new-product manager must maintain close contact with the top executive—occasional formal talks and frequent informal chats. The president is the man in charge. But he is a man. He will have his preconceptions and opinions. When he makes a decision—or decides not to make a decision—it will be for very human reasons. The new-product manager must learn to know this man. The most logical, persuasive, powerful and appealing presentation will not sway him one iota if it runs contrary to his own experience and inclinations. There is no point in the new-product head wasting his time on projects which will be turned down. And he has to know the president well enough to know what will be approved. If the president has strong preferences, it is obvious that it is along these directions that the new-product manager should first explore. There is no excuse in the world for the manager and his own superior to be at cross purposes. This is not only self defeating, it is suicidal.

But when the new-product manager has good rapport with his boss, if the projects which the manager suggests are enthusiastically received, then everything involved with internal development goes easily. And this includes the delegated authority necessary to consummate the plans. When the president is enthusiastic, the word quickly spreads down the chain of command and the new-product manager will have little difficulty in getting cooperation from the department heads. Sometimes the approval is a grudging or a disinterested one, forced by an irrefutable presentation. In this case the new-product manager lost while winning, because he will have his problems to overcome.

Just remember that getting along with the boss means selling that which is salable—in short, a personal marketing job. Once he is on target, a sharp new-product manager should be able both to sell his new-product proposals—and to deliver.

HOW TO SPOT A DRY HOLE

Unfortunately, not all firms who talk new products are actually willing—or able—to live with a deliberate effort. The problem is inherent in business: often words, phrases, titles are used when their use is not supported by fact. Marketing is an "in" word—and has been for years. Yet the basic concepts of marketing are found much less frequently than the widespread use of the word would suggest. All too many firms updated their image by changing the sales manager's title to marketing manager. Same man, same job, same methods—but now the firm does "marketing." Such examples are legion and accepted as part of corporate life by experienced management people.

But the younger or newer management man may find these facts of life unnerving if he does not anticipate them. The deplorable statistics of new-product development prove that most companies who talk the process are unwilling to invest the effort required. And since a profitable new-product program is a long-term effort, requiring both cooperation and active participation by much of top management and most of the department heads, there is just no way in which one man can succeed if the environment is not receptive. So if you are new in your position, spend some portion of your first few months in an objective appraisal of the company and its management.

Some presidents like to play cat-and-mouse games, setting up one department as an irritant or check against other departments, and thereby eliminating the interdepartmental cooperation which is essential. Occasionally a president has little actual knowledge of his firm's product or markets. Such men may have come to power through inheritance, or appointment from outside. They may be very capable generalists or extreme specialists (attorneys, accountants) but the dangerous characteristic is that such a man may not be able to objectively select between conflicting technical opinions—and may make his decisions along personality lines. It is not impossible to implement a serious new-product program under such a president—but it is most difficult.

Two other corporate climates can scuttle the program: an excessively political climate and advanced corporate senility. In the former case, little gets done because nobody trusts anybody else; cooperation is impossible. But corporate lethargy is more prevalent—a company and its people become so tied to routine and policy that a concerted effort in a new direction is impossible. The climate is characterized by extreme politeness, glowing visions of future growth, a willingness to agree to any program—but no deadlines, no assigned responsibilities, no unpleasant whipcracking, and no progress.

If mountains are movable, make plans for moving them. But if they are immovable, look for a more productive firm. Do not wait it out, hoping that things will improve, or that certain executives will retire. If you dwell too long in even the most frustrating climate, eventually you will put down roots, adopt the firm's philosophies and procedures as your own, and whatever abilities and talents you may possess will be lost among the quickly-passing years.

When you find yourself in a blind alley, quit and look elsewhere.

Ideas Worth Exploring--No. 2

VISES AND ACCESSORIES

No firm appears to have done a thorough job of exploring the various types of vises and accessories which might be marketed successfully. Yet the vast majority of relatively low-production tooling could be replaced by well-designed vises and suitable accessories. Among the sketches are angular vise jaws, high-rise jaws for edge operations on wide workpieces, three stop designs for repetitive part location, and a device for cross drilling round stock.

Extender jaws broaden the range of a vise for light-duty work. A compound vise could be used for working on a row of thin workpieces. The gang vise shown should provide more pieces per day than the familiar arrangement of two independent fixtures at the opposite ends of the milling-machine table, climb milling one workpiece and conventional milling on the other. The indexing arrangement would speed drilling, reaming, and broaching operations.

The point is that variations on the basic vise theme are almost endless. A good concept might incorporate a basic vise, available in a wide range of sizes. It could be provided with an interchangeable screw, hydraulic, or hydro-pneumatic clamping arrangement.

Marketing Comments: If the vise is well designed and reasonably priced, the potential market should be substantial. Prospects include all industry (though manufacturing is highest, of course), service and repair firms—even the home handyman. The overall potential depends only upon the ingenuity of the design, the price, advertising, and distribution. When one considers the total volume in bench vises, pipe vises, and machinist's vises presently sold by the many thousands of industrial distributors—and the thought that a marketable accessory line might double or triple this amount, the opportunities become attractive.

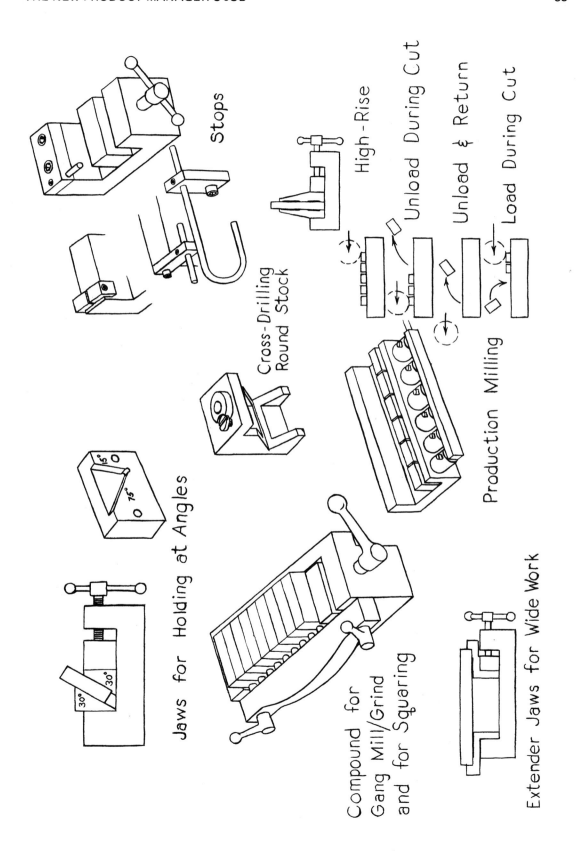

Stops

High-Rise

Unload During Cut

Unload & Return

Load During Cut

Cross-Drilling
Round Stock

Production Milling

Jaws for Holding at Angles

Compound for
Gang Mill/Grind
and for Squaring

Extender Jaws for Wide Work

Chapter 4
Getting Started

> ... the first step in establishing a functioning new-product development program is to determine the firm's market history, where it stands now, and the natural direction of its development. This study identifies the most likely market and identifies the scope of potential new products. Specific new product prospects quickly appear—and the ones which can be made profitable most quickly are the ones to start with.

WHERE ARE YOU NOW?

A corporation is a living organism. With only rare exceptions, every company is moving in some direction, constantly changing (if slowly). New-product development is part of this movement. The pace may be accelerated but great leaps forward are seldom possible, nor are abrupt changes of direction. If your company is a conservative maker of automobile accessories, you will not be successful developing and marketing an automatic can opener for the housewife. The profitable new product is most likely to be one which lies in the path of the firm's natural movement.

In order to determine the direction of this movement, create a plot of where the firm is today and where it came from, as shown in Figure 4-1. Start with a thorough analysis of the product line and the markets now being served. Determine which products go into which markets; as much as possible, do this with precision. On the surface, if one market is wood furniture manufacturing, it makes no difference whether the customer makes bassinets or television consoles. However, when it becomes time to dig deeply for market analysis or for names of customers and prospects, it makes a great deal of difference, so keep the market categories narrow. Furthermore, if you can determine the percent of sales volume going to each market, you are better able to

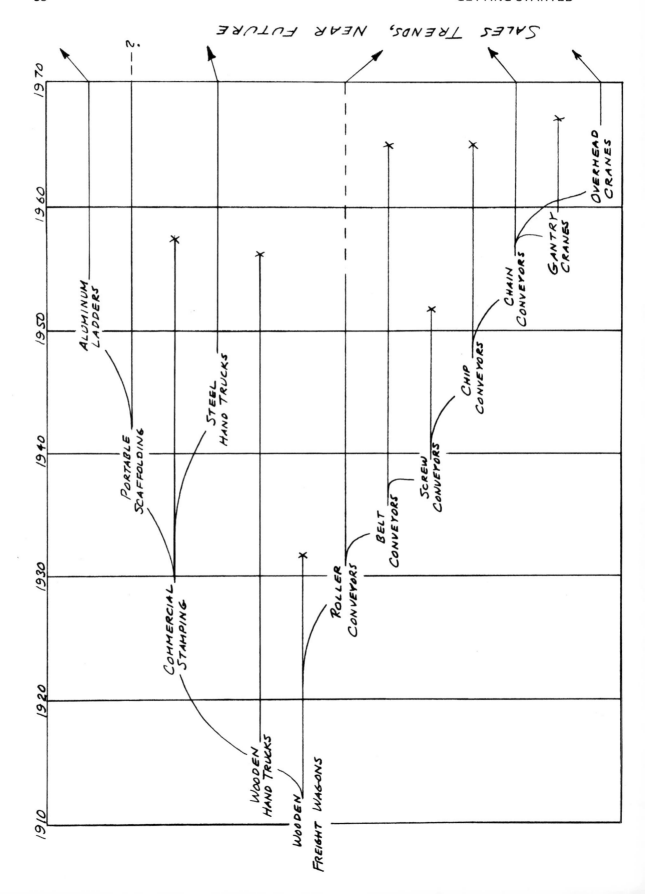

analyze the firm's accomplishments, growth rates, and potentials. So attempt as fine a breakdown as possible.

The best way to develop the data is to obtain the opinions and estimates of people in the sales department, regional sales managers, salesmen, service men, and others who might know. It is not at all necessary to do a vast amount of digging in the billing department (and if you sell through distributors, this would probably be fruitless anyway). An averaging of the intelligent estimates of men who know the markets involved is accurate enough for the purpose at hand.

If a wide product line and a number of different markets are involved, the best way to organize the data is with an input/output chart, as in Figures 4-2A and 4-2B. Across the top list the markets served, and down the left side list the products. Arrange both listings in some orderly sequence, with related listings adjacent. Trace each product across the chart, checking the columns for the applicable markets. The indication could be merely an "X," showing activity. But indicating ranking, percentages, annual sales volume, etc., is more useful. The chart portrays the nature of the product/market mix—whether the company is making a number of closely related products for a narrow market, a wide group of products for one market, closely related products for numerous markets, or a spread in both directions.

With most companies, there is a strong clustering within the product line—or among the markets served. Corporations are directed by men, and very few men have broad enough personal experience to carry a company into a host of different markets with a number of non-related product lines. It may have a wide product line or a host of markets, but seldom both. Additionally, the practical requirements of engineering experience and selling tend to keep a company along restricted paths. When a company becomes too widely spread, a few product lines or markets are pushed heavily and the others are largely ignored.

Figure 4-1

A time plot of a firm's products shows its direction of marketing movement, including abandoned items. This is the same firm discussed in Figure 2-1B, but elaborated upon. As before, product growth in the material handling line has been toward high value, heavily engineered, system sales products such as overhead conveyors and cranes. However, war-time expansion into contract stamping led to development of portable scaffolding and later to aluminum ladders, the ladders being sold primarily through large mail-order consumer outlets.

A plot of this type makes it easy for a new-product manager to determine the direction(s) of natural movement. Possible new products can be fitted to see if they are within the evident interest areas of a firm. Notice, however, that the ladders are not a product as such, but merely a natural outgrowth of the commercial stamping department, almost completely divorced from engineering and normal sales activity. One could thus surmise that any large-volume but simple product, primarily stamped and assembled, would be of interest as long as the same customers were involved.

On the opposite leg, the movement would indicate a future interest in overhead storage systems, warehouse stacking systems, and other systems requiring normal growth of engineering ability, but without a marketing shift. Particularly notice that the firm stays with products which do not require sophisticated machine design or structural engineering (as would be involved in high-tonnage cranes), and that the firm is a follower, making products pioneered by others.

Figure 4-2A

Products \ Markets	Rail Roads	General Indust. Distributors	Short-Line Indust. Dist.	Material Handling Dist.	Mat'l Handlg. Mfg. Reps.	Automotive – OEM	Automotive – Plant	Chemical Processing	Food Processing	Meat Packing	Building Contractors	Contractors' Supply Dist.	Consumer Mail Order	Born	Died	Trend
Freight Wagons	1	2		3										1910	1932	
Wooden Hand Trucks	4	5												1913	1956	
Metal Hand Trucks	6	7	8	9								10	11	1944	–	↗
Gravity Roller Conv.			12	13	14									1928	–	↗
Powered Belt Conv.			15	16	17		18	19	20	21		22		1933	1965	
Screw Conveyors				23	24			25	26			27		1938	1952	
Chip Conveyors				28	29		30							1946	1965	
O'Head Chain Conv.				31	32		33	34	35	36				1953	–	↗
Gantry Cranes				37	38		39							1958	1967	
O'Head Trav. Cranes				40	41		42							1963	–	↗
Commercial Stampings						43								1925	1958	
Portable Scaffolding	44	45	46	47	48		49				50	51	52	1939	–	?
Aluminum Step Ladders	53	54	55	56	57		58				59	60	61	1951	–	↗

Figure 4-2A

Here is a product/market input/output chart for the product line in Figure 4-1. The boxes are numbered for reference, the assumption being that the analyst has notes for each box, numbered to agree. A different picture emerges from that shown in Figure 4-1 and the market emphasis permits refining the new-product guesses. In particular, the firm has virtually abandoned its original railroad and industrial-distributor customers and has shifted heavily to material-handling specialists.

The direct sales to automotive firms and their suppliers is healthy but is beginning to shoot out into virgin territory—chemicals and food plants. Between Figure 4-1 and this one, the directions of natural growth are quite evident.

60

	40 MAT'L HNDLG DISTRIBUTORS	41 MAT'L HNDLG MFG. REPS	42 AUTO AND AUTO –PART PLANTS
OVERHEAD TRAVELING CRANES 2-10 TON	Started 1964 $M Sales '65 80 '70 265 '75 (410)	Started 1963 $M Sales '65 1,135 '70 2,690 '75 (2,760)	Started 1963 $M Sales '65 630 '70 1,080 '75 (1,800)
	NOTES: REPLACE WITH MR's IN BETTER AREAS. ONLY TWO DISTRIBS ARE DOING GOOD JOB. SEARCH OUT OTHER DISTRIBS INTERESTED IN ENGINEERED SYSTEMS SALES? TRAVELING SCHOOL TO TEACH DISTRIB M-H SALESMEN?	NOTES: SOME PRESSURE FOR MORE ADVANCED SYSTEMS AND HEAVIER TONNAGES (TO 30 TON). NEED MORE/FASTER HELP FROM OUR SALES/ SERVICE ENGINEERS. RUN ENGINEERING SCHOOL FOR MR's? SPEED UP OUR QUOTING PROCESS—LOSING SOME BUSINESS BECAUSE BID WAS LATE. PUSH MR's INTO WIDER MARKET AREAS.	NOTES: CUSTOMER'S NEEDS INCLUDE MORE AUTOMATIC SYSTEMS—INCLUDING N/C PROGRAMMED IN-PROCESS STORAGE AND RETRIEVAL THRU INTER-FACE WITH CHAIN CONVEYOR. EXPLORE FEASIBILITY. LITTLE NEED FOR HIGHER SPEEDS—SOME FOR MORE TONNAGE.

Figure 4-2B

Typical notes for developing the input/output chart—and for supporting the crystal ball which is expected to predict likely new-product ventures.

Now expand the product/market chart by adding the time element. Determine the year of introduction for each product line, and try to learn when the product penetrated each of its markets. Supplement this with dollar values—average sales volume for the last two years and for a decade ago for each product/market box. The chart now shows which products are supporting the company, which ones are growing rapidly, which are stagnant, and which are dying on the vine. These failing products may be tempting prospects for salvage—or they may be excellent things to leave alone.

The new-product manager's job is to accelerate the company's growth—not attempt to turn it around. The direction and rate of growth can be seen in a chart showing product/market/time. The movement of the company over a span of years can become even more apparent if you track down products which have been dropped from the line and indicate them in appropriate boxes on the chart. It is safe to assume that re-entry to markets which were abandoned would be resisted by many within the company. The future lies in the empty boxes and beyond the ends of the lists.

WHERE ARE YOU GOING?

An historical analysis of a company's marketing activities is useful. It tells the new-product manager a great deal about the company and permits him to project its movement ahead. By forecasting likely types of new products and new markets, the new-product activity can be on, or quite close to, the company's inherent path of movement.

There is a definite advantage in being close to the natural target in projecting the company's growth. One of these is that when the new-product manager casually suggests exploring a type of product, it is almost certain to have been thought of before. This puts the new-product manager in the position of agreeing with the preconceived notions of others; usually a good position to achieve.

An analysis of the penetration for each product should be made, as in Figures 4-3A and 4-3B. Do not attempt to do this for each product/market box—it is too much work and is of real value only in advanced market analysis and sales forecasting. Start by finding the total dollar volume of a given product, as made by your firm and all of its competitors. Data is available from the government and other sources which gives annual sales volume for various products, sometimes even by state or region. Data for each of a number of years can be used to determine which products are rapidly growing, which are standing still, and which are declining. By playing your own firm's sales volume for a given product against that of the industry, the firm's penetration rate for each year is obtained. This penetration rate tells how well the company fares in relationship to its competitors and is an extremely significant figure. Over a few years, every company either gains on or loses out to competitors. Changes in penetration rate tell much about customer acceptance of the company's products, its quality/delivery/price as compared with competition, and even gives some insight into the effectiveness of the sales staff.

Another logical study to make is a product/market breakdown of profit per product line. In most companies, however, it lacks meaning and is next to impossible to do anyway. First of all, no one is likely to have any accurate figures for relative profit by market for a given product. Worse yet, the average company does not even know which products (as such) are most profitable. To be sure, accounting can quickly give you profit figures by product line. But for long-term planning, such numbers are meaningless in most cases because of the interdependence of profit and volume.

Usually a company derives the majority of its profit from its large-volume products. However, the high-volume product is the one in which the company has invested the most time and effort—production facilities are the best the company can arrange, inventory control is the most sophisticated, and the sales force finds this product comfortable to sell. Volume brings profit—or perhaps profit attracts the effort necessary to achieve volume.

Conversely, a product showing little or no profit may actually be profitless—but it is also likely to be made with the oldest machinery, on tooling that has not been updated

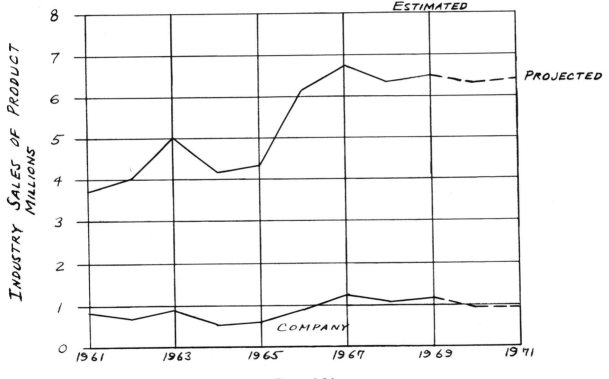

Figure 4-3A

Company sales volume, as plotted against industry total sales for the product involved. The industry sales volume can be obtained from the U.S. Department of Commerce/Business and Defense Services Administration reports, industry associations, and magazine publishers in the field.

The firm involved here has an excessive susceptibility to the sales fluctuations of the industry. This implies that the firm is second choice with its leading customers; in bad years it is the first dropped and in good years it gets business which the competition cannot handle. Its product/price/delivery mix (or perhaps its sales force) is holding it back. Compare with the plot in Figure 4-3B.

for years, and to be a product which the sales department ignores. Of course profits are slim. Products which have a poor profit showing are trapped by their own condition—the lack of profit means that there are no funds available for the investments necessary to reduce costs, increase sales, and capture the missing profits. So get the profit figures, but do not take them too seriously.

By the time the new-product manager has gathered this data and thought about what it tells him, he should have an excellent grasp of the company's marketing condition. He knows a great deal about the company, its direction, and which products and markets are most likely to become of interest.

KNOW YOUR COMPETITION

A company does not exist alone. For almost every manufacturer, there are competitors making directly comparable products. Even when the company (by virtue of patents or some other protective situation) has an exclusive on a certain product, competitors will make the products which are alternate solutions to the same application. Occasionally, a company has a policy of ignoring the competition, working

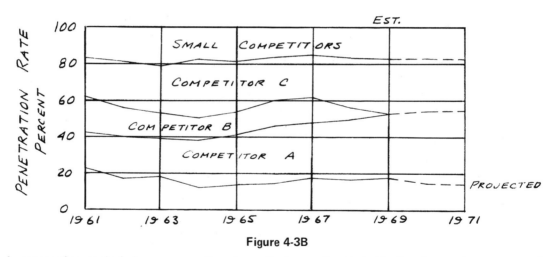

Figure 4-3B

A penetration analysis is more revealing. In particular, notice that this firm is too slow to react. In good years it moves too slowly to take advantage of available business and in bad years it is too slow to sharpen its pencil and intensify its sales efforts. When Competitor B dropped out of the race, everybody benefitted except the firm involved. The overall penetration rate is marginally upward—unless the period from 1961 to 1969 is a cycle, with a new low coming.

Based upon this history, one would suggest a thorough analysis of the product and its delivery as compared with competition. If these are in line and published prices are competitive, suspicion would focus on the use of unpublished discounts by competitors. Perhaps they have much broader product lines, more active advertising, or a more aggressive sales force.

In a very real sense, this is none of the new-product manager's business. And this is true. Nonetheless, any ills that befall the present products will also affect any new products—and anticipated problems can be dealt with better than those that are unexpected.

strictly on a "damn the torpedoes, full speed ahead" theory. This is brave but not necessarily wise. Keeping an eye on the competition can tell you a great deal about your markets and how well you do what you are doing.

For instance, it is simple to obtain an index to the productivity of your factory. Make up a list of the competitors and determine the number of employees for each. This can be found in various directories, government statistics, and D&B reports. Divide the total sales volume for the industry by the number of employees in the industry and you get dollars of sales volume per employee—a rough estimate of industry productivity. Do the same arithmetic on your own firm and you have a quick guide to your company's relative efficiency. Sometimes this is interesting.

The first step in building a file on competitors is to secure their catalogs and price lists. This is done easily enough, usually just by writing to them. Some firms automatically send copies of new literature to their competitors, as a courtesy gesture. This is probably carrying gentlemanliness too far—yet requests for literature among competitors are normally honored, if for no reason other than the value of reciprocation. However, if a competitor is coy, there are all sorts of ways of getting catalogs, including picking them up from distributors, having the salesmen filch them from friendly purchasing agent's desks, even using magazine "bingo" cards under assumed names. In any case, build a complete file of competitors' catalogs and price lists.

Then look into each competitor's firm. If his stock is traded actively, any stock broker can obtain financial statements for you. Most companies subscribe to Dun & Bradstreet or some other credit reporting firm These provide in-depth reports on any company at very low cost. The reports are of interest because they provide a history of the company and the background of its top management. However, accuracy tends to be low since each firm tells D&B what it wants them to know. Further, if the competitor is a division of a larger corporation, part of a conglomerate, or if the competitor has an extremely wide product line, such reports tell you little about the product at hand. Deeper digging is necessary to turn up the information required or to create useful estimates.

To pin down data on a single product made by a multi-product competitor, first get state statistics on manufacture of the product (this is usually census data). Then get D&B or similar figures for all the single-product competitors in the state. Subtract them from the total, which leaves only the one or two larger firms standing. Estimates of the breakdown between the few large firms will then usually suffice. Intelligence is interesting and potentially valuable. It is also time consuming and must be adjusted to the value of the information gained.

There is a very useful result for all this work. If the company begins to push for greater sales volume of a given product or in a given market, they will immediately affect the competition. Gains in market penetration are achieved at the competitors' expense, by moving harder and faster and by taking advantage of their weaknesses and mistakes. Analyzing your firm's opportunities involves forecasting—careful, objective, educated guesses as to how successful a given effort will be. The forecasts are accurate in direct ratio to your firm's collective knowledge of the competition. At best, forecasting is risky, yet a large part of a new-product manager's time will be spent in working with forecasts. It is needlessly hazardous to make them in the face of ignorance about competitors.

Learn about your company, learn about your markets, and learn about your competitors. Market ignorance leads to all kinds of hazardous situations—including dangerous complacency. It is not at all unusual to find a company, perfectly happy with an annual 5% sales growth, suddenly wise up to the fact that the industry as a whole has been growing at 10%—with a resulting steady attrition of their penetration. And penetration, once lost, is most difficult to regain.

WHAT DO YOU HAVE TO WORK WITH?

Your company, as it stands, is completely preoccupied with doing what it is doing—making and selling its existing products. All the department heads are wrapped up in this task; from chief inspector to president, everyone spends his time and makes his living in working with these products. And both customers and prospects see your company in terms of these products. Anything the new-product manager may hope to do will be affected by the firm's present product line.

The company today may be a great asset to any new products it might develop—but this is not very likely. In most cases, the hoped-for gains from new products are endangered or retarded by the history of the existing ones. This is not to say that every company's product line is a marketing liability—it is just that employee thinking becomes stereotyped, and so does the thinking of customers. If a company is extremely progressive, dominating all its markets with top-caliber products, each one loaded with exclusive features and sold with both delivery and price advantages, then the market's reaction to such a firm will be to welcome the introduction of new products. However, if (as is usually the case) the company makes products which range from the very best offered to mediocre, with competitive deliveries and competitive prices (that is, better than some competitors and worse than others), then the market will have a mixed reaction to the introduction of a new product. The new-product manager must learn how mixed this reaction is. So the next step is to do a complete and thorough analysis of the firm's existing products.

Compare each product with that of the competition. Are your firm's products as good (better/worse)? Are the sales features true as claimed? Do they have significance to the customer? Do the products have any exclusive sales features? Does the competition exaggerate sales features—or make unrealistic claims? Determine your company's policies as to product descriptions and sales features in their catalogs and verbal presentations. How conservative are the claims? You don't want to oversell or make false claims, but it is foolish to hide one's light under a bushel. Advertising and sales policies which apply to existing products will almost certainly apply to new products—or you will have to fight for changes.

If your firm has tended to ignore the competition, to be disdainful of it, friendly with it, or just plain ignorantly complacent, you may find that the company actually has little knowledge of how good its products are or how they compare with competitive offerings. Where practical, buy the products of competitors and run tests. Do not ignore the small competitors—often the best and newest ideas are being brewed in these small firms. If tests are impractical, try to see the competitor's products in use, by a customer. If even that is impractical, talk to your salesmen; they should know. The intrinsic value of your products greatly affects the marketability of the company name—makes it either a plus factor or a minus factor for any new products you may introduce.

Compare the range of sizes, capacities, styles, etc. Does your firm make a short line, a comparable line, or the widest line? There is always a definite sales advantage in having the widest range of sizes or capacities. Even if a customer prefers a competitor's product, he will often come to you if you make sizes which nobody else offers. As an alternate approach, you might make only one size but, by specializing, provide much better quality/price/delivery. Either way your salesmen have a door opener, something exclusive to talk about.

A company with an abbreviated product line is lazy. It hopes to concentrate on the large volume, gravy customers (where everybody else concentrates, too—so price is the only real consideration), and leave the hard work and odd-ball applications to others. In good times the short product line may maximize profits by reducing sales costs, but it makes it very difficult to combat aggressive competition, and an abbreviated product line emasculates your sales pitch.

Look into the specifics of your company's distribution channels. How effective are they as compared with methods used by competition? How enthusiastic are the firm's salesmen (outside *and* inside); are they a red-hot group, or are there strong undertones of disillusion and frustration? An enthusiastic sales force is easily wound up to run with a new product. A tired sales force will sleep through any new product and a completely different distribution may be necessary for getting sales volume built up.

Find out how the company's products fare with competitive offerings from a standpoint of design engineering, quality control, price, delivery, warranties, etc. Again, company accomplishments, faux pas, and policies will certainly affect the success of new products. The new-product manager should make arrangements to spend a few days on the road with company salesmen—preferably, salesmen far afield, not home-office men. The idea is to listen; you will meet a few customers and distributors, but this is beside the point. The real objective is to find out what the outside salesmen think of the company, its products and its policies. They are company men—but advance troops. They *know* your customers—the people at the home office *know about* customers. In fact, these salesmen (far away from head-quarters' influence) are probably the only people in the entire company who see it through the customer's eyes. Do not talk new products—what you want to learn is how good the company is, and how customers react to it. A few such trips will tell you.

Back at the ranch again, get acquainted with the factory. Study what (and how modern) the methods are, how the products are made, how modern the facilities are, and how good quality control is. Talk with the tool and manufacturing engineers and find out their batting average when they try to sell new ideas. Top management deaf to recommendations by conscientious factory people will probably have a tin ear for you, too. Further, a company unwilling to keep its production facilities up to date incurs high costs and handicaps its entire product line. This handicap will probably apply to any new products, also. Therefore, a new product must be viewed critically to see how amenable it is to being manufactured under such circumstances.

If a company is unwilling to invest in modern production facilities, the only way around this impasse is to buy all or much of the work outside. See if top management and the department heads have any strong feelings or policies on this. Generally, farming out work makes everybody feel uncomfortable; the human tendency is to feel that if work is done under one's own roof it will be done right—or at least you can watch it going wrong. If you farm the work out, you lose control—pricing, delivery, quality, profits, etc. Yet if a company's production facilities are manifestly incapable of making the new product, the idea will either have to be abandoned or farmed out. Beware of firm roadblocks in this direction.

IMPROVING THE ODDS

The research described is the new-product manager's homework. From it he learns about the company, its past and present successes and failures, and gains a good idea of how the company got where it is, the likelihood of it going farther, and clues as to the direction of that growth. This knowledge reinforces the new-product manager's concept of his position and his estimated chances of winning. It adds flesh to top management's stated thoughts about new-product development. If his top management defined their area of new-product interest as anything in material handling, yet he finds that the product line has never included anything successful other than casters, a contradictory situation exists—and the neophyte manager must tread softly until he finds out what the score is.

The next step is actual new-product development. However, before leaping wildly ahead, take another look at the analyses of the company's product/market mix. In this data may lie excellent opportunities for successful product development—to be sure, not new products in the sense of inventing the light bulb, but new products in the sense of something new for the sales force to talk about. The charts should have shown places where the company had an abbreviated product line, products that have not kept abreast of competitive engineering developments, etc. Each of these is an opportunity.

Statistics tell us that well over 90% of all new products fail. That is to say, that some 95% of the time the new-product development man or staff did a miserable job. This is disheartening. Presumably an unsuccessful new-product manager gets some credit for playing the game right, even if he loses. But there is a great deal more satisfaction to be derived from winning—if for no other reason than that it eliminates the inconvenience of job hunting. It is not really important whether it is a big win or a small win, as long as the first venture is successful.

The odds are fantastically in favor of a new product venture's success when it is a simple addition, expansion, updating, or correction of the existing product line. It is in this direction that the new-product manager should first set his sights. If it is known in the company that new products are his area, he will have been inundated by ideas—good, bad, indifferent, and intriguing. Accept them, smile, and quietly shelve them. You need some carefully selected preliminary wins before the main bout.

WHAT IS A NEW PRODUCT?

Like too many other business phrases, "new-product development" has been used and misused until it has become meaningless—or has acquired so many shadings of meaning that it has nearly lost its usefulness. Since no substitute exists, this is unfortunate. However, in a language where "a fat chance" and "a slim chance" mean the same thing, it follows that a phrase like "new-product development" can mean almost anything. Momentarily ignoring the word "development" (which is reasonably unambiguous) we can define, for the purpose of this book, the meaning of "new product."

> *New Product*—noun; any thing, or closely related group of things (products), which is not presently being sold, or which is presently being sold but where only an insignificant portion of the potential sales volume has been achieved.

Thus, a "new" product can be one which *no* one has ever made before or perhaps even thought of. It can be one which no one is presently selling. It can be one which some other firm or firms sell but which has unexploited sales potential. It can be one which other firms are selling in volume, but which your firm does not sell. And it can be a product which you now sell but which your firm has not developed to its full sales potential; a product which is new only in the sense that it is not a factor in your dealings with the majority of your customers. If it does not loom large in relation to other products in your sales analysis, and it could be made to do so, it can be processed as a "new product."

This reasoning brings us to an easy discovery—there are three classes of new products:

1. The not-thought-of idea, or the thought-of-but-not-made product, which is "new" to everybody.
2. The product which is not new to the world but is new to your firm.
3. The product which is not new to your firm but is new to most of the customers who should buy it.

Considered in reverse order, as in Figure 4-4, these three classes of new products actually represent different levels of development or maturity and need increasing amounts of work to bring them to a profitable level:

1. The neglected product needs analysis and exploitation.
2. The product which your firm does not sell (but others do) requires analysis, development, reanalysis, and exploitation.
3. The nonexistent product requires discovery, analysis, development, reanalysis, and exploitation.

In this book all three classes of new products are discussed, because a real profit maker could be found in any of the three. For the neophyte new-product manager, the neglected product—existing but presently unexploited—is the best one to start with. It

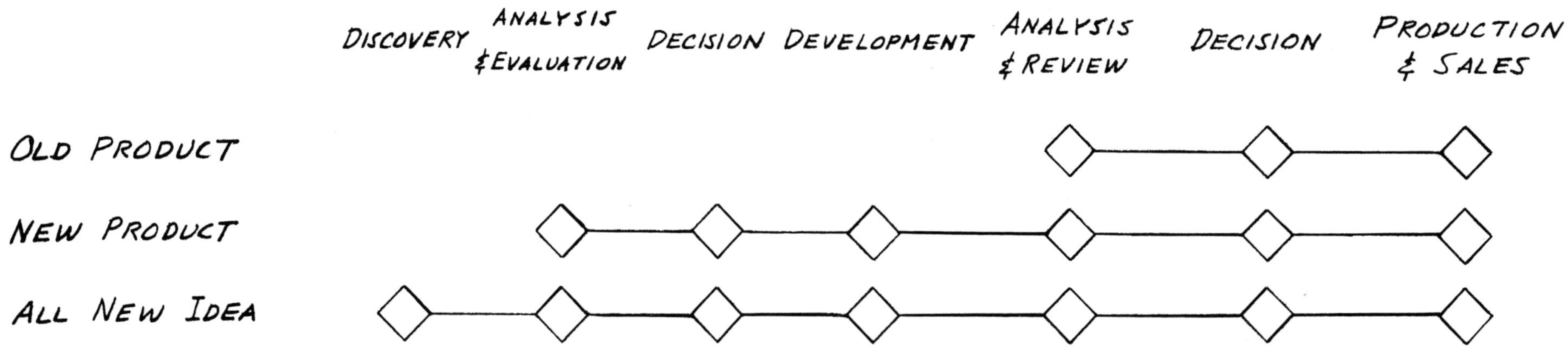

Figure 4-4

The principal steps in new-product development, for the three classes of new products. The neophyte new-product manager is urged to concentrate on resurrecting old products first: there is less work, less risk, and the results are known more quickly.

represents fewer unknown quantities, much less work is required, and results come much faster. Becoming a competitor of other presently active firms represents the next level of increasing difficulty, guesswork, risk, investment (probably), and time lag between green light and anticipated profit levels. Obviously, starting from absolute zero is the most arduous route of all.

There is a reason why so many new products fail: known, developable products are bypassed because the unknown offers more challenge, appeal, romance, or imagined potential. Treasure hunting offers great possibilities but correspondingly poor odds. The author does not intend to belittle the importance of pioneering a new idea, or the huge financial rewards that accrue when this is well timed and successfully accomplished. But the objective of the process is profitable products—with the word profitable coming first. And that is where profit considerations should be—first.

Most references on new-product development completely ignore the existing but unexploited product, considering it merely a sales-department problem. Yet if the product is unexploited, then manufacturing, sales, and/or management have missed the boat. And since the new-product manager's task consists of nurse-maiding potentially profitable products through these three groups of people, rescuing the neglected product fits neatly into his operations. Before adding new products to your catalog, make certain that you are making full potential of the ones within its pages.

Ideas Worth Exploring--No. 3

ABRASIVE CUT-OFF MACHINES

Description: The familiar abrasive cut-off machine in most of its forms, particularly with smaller bench or pedestal-mounted units.

Marketing Comments: The abrasive cut-off machine is made by a host of firms, large and small. Most of the makers are relatively small firms, with designs that tend to be long on price and short on quality and engineering. While there is plenty of competition, the market appears wide open for a well-designed line, with machines in a range of sizes, priced in proportion to their cost and value, and marketed in volume—preferably through an established distribution system.

The first necessary step is a thorough survey of the field to see who makes what. Then do a careful engineering analysis of each design—its strengths and weaknesses. A financial study of the various firms will provide data on the size of the market.

The abrasive cut-off machine (which has been around for years) has never been given the thought or engineering which was applied to band saws and reciprocating saws many years ago. From a cursory inspection, it appears that there is a void between the smaller units and the larger production models. Further, well-made smaller units could be equipped with automatic stock feed for production cutting of lighter bars.

There are at least two major markets: manufacturing (metalworking of all kinds, some plastics, ceramics and many nonmetallics), and construction (for on-site cutting of bricks, ceramic tile, and similar products).

This is a marketing opportunity well worth looking into.

(Illustration appears on the following page.)

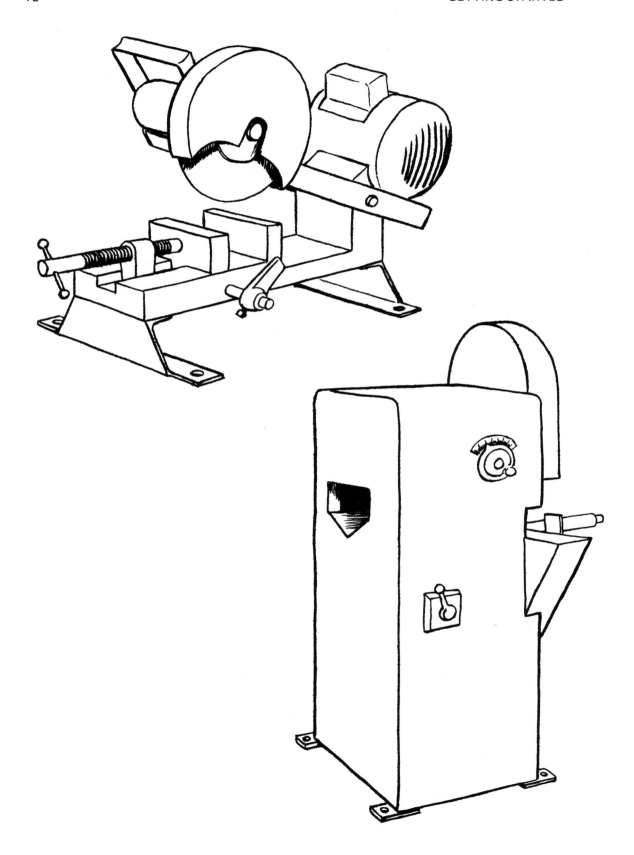

SECTION II

The New Product Development Process

Chapter 5

Generating Fresh Profits from Old New Products

> . . . the best product for the neophyte new-product manager
> is the one which can be brought to the profitable level most
> readily; it is folly to launch a vast long-term project when
> there are less risky, short-term projects available. This chapter
> analyzes the "old" new product, how to find it, and how to
> bring it to a profitable level.

EENIE, MEENIE, MINIE, MOE

In the previous chapter it was suggested that the new-product manager make a thorough product/market/volume/penetration/profit analysis of his company. Such a study pinpoints those products which are doing well—and those which are not. Among those which contribute little or nothing to the company profit will be found all kinds of dogs and orphans: those in the declining phase of their life cycle, some which were poorly designed, products with poor market acceptance, products with little profit potential but carried as a "customer service," etc. Others were delivered to the sales department and dumped there or had fouled-up introductions—the purely neglected products and those which never got off the ground.

The object is to find products which have all the earmarks of success and yet have not achieved their full potential.

If formal new-product development is new to the firm it is important that the neophyte new-product manager make a good showing quickly—win the first time at bat. There is no better, faster, or easier way of doing this than to find a suitable neglected product for which there is good potential, develop a thorough sales and promotion program, put it into effect, and thus convert a nonproductive product into one which contributes significantly to the company's profits and overall health. The trick is in finding the "suitable" product.

For some of the poor performers, reasons can be quickly found—poor design, obsolete product, very limited industry sales, noncompetitive price, poor delivery, etc. And yet the study is almost certain to reveal others which show no self-evident reasons for their lack of success. Make a list of them. Then add the products which appear held back purely because of noncompetitive price or delivery. If any product already has a penetration rate of 20% or so, cross it off the list since the market is too small to bother with. If any of the products require major redesign or modernizing, eliminate these also—they are Class 2 new products, as described in the following chapter, and a great deal more work is involved. The remaining ones are prospects for treatment as old new products.

They will share a number of faults—very small market penetration, sales volume at an unsatisfactory level, noncompetitive prices, poor delivery, neglect by the sales staff, exclusion from advertising programs, etc. But each one "feels good." Compare each of them with competitive offerings, to satisfy yourself that the company's product is a good one—that it has no functional or design defects.

From this collection of product misfits, pick two or three that look good, that you can become enthusiastic about.

20/20 HINDSIGHT

Develop a thorough history for each of the selected products, both in the company and as an industry. Find out all circumstances of the birth of the firm's products and what took place immediately afterwards. Neglected products seem to share certain experiences. In most cases, the now-neglected product started out looking good and was so mishandled in its early stages that the sales force and customers lost interest. Analyzing these birth defects tells the beginning new-product manager a great deal. Particularly, it gives him a road map to failure—a specific list of the things to avoid in profitable new-product development. This can be extremely useful when he is ready to introduce a genuinely new product into the market place.

Ask questions—track down each product's original champions—the men who were behind the idea, pushed it through development, landed the first few sales, and were bitterly frustrated by its poor beginnings. Get their opinions about what went wrong. Then talk with others in production, advertising, sales, and the inside and field sales staffs. Some of the tales of woe collected will be disgusting, some astonishing, some sickening, and some genuinely funny.

Usually the champions became so incensed about how others mistreated their baby that they dropped out, preferring to be no longer involved. But their bitterness is a thin disguise for the remnants of their interest—and if you can convince them that this time things will be done properly, you can tap their experience, expertise, and enthusiasm.

The commonest causes of new-product miscarriage are insufficient sales effort in the early stages or going after sales prematurely—both proof of poor planning. The lack of deliberate sales development of a new product will stunt its growth. During the first few years a new product requires intensive sales and service effort—far beyond what can be justified by the volume or profits realized. It is difficult for the sales department to provide this extraordinary effort. With the product's original champions in a huff, there is nobody pushing for sales. And the mishandled new product goes nowhere—a result of a bad introduction and subsequent malnutrition.

The other common variety is where the product goes to market prematurely. The prototypes are approved, advertising is started, sales meetings are held, and the salesmen start to bring in orders. But just as production is started, defects are found. Everything stops for quickie repairs. Meantime, customers and salesmen lose interest. Months pass and the champions of the idea, busily correcting as they go along, finally have the product ready for the market place. But by that time nobody is interested.

Sometimes poor coordination or simple misunderstandings does a product in. One company developed an excellent small timing motor which required new production facilities. The equipment was purchased with an anticipated payoff period of 36 months. Long before the three years were up, the capacity was oversold and a bad delivery situation developed as business flowed in.

But the financial people in the company had not been properly briefed on the nature of the o.e.m. (original equipment manufacturer) market and they refused to approve purchase of additional machinery until the original equipment had been paid off. Most of the profits had gone into inventory building, so the firm's financial people stood adamant. Deliveries became progressively worse, customers began to look elsewhere, salesmen turned their attention to other products, and finally the production capacity was adequate after all. By the time the payoff period was over, nobody in the sales department was interested in expansion. In this case, the company had a live one and was unable to believe its own good fortune.

New products acquired through purchase of small companies frequently feed the statistics. The purchase is handled by the financial or legal department. Naturally, everything is hush-hush until the deal goes through, so neither market research nor sales planning can be done. One day the trucks roll in full of machinery and somebody (usually the advertising manager) is sent scurrying for a desk for the ex-president. The little company is absorbed clumsily by its large and essentially disinterested purchaser. Product quality, delivery, and pricing suffer; most of the small firm's steady customers are lost. The management and engineers of the purchased firm give up in disgust and leave. The big company generates no champions for the product, and by the time it is finally integrated smoothly into the firm's operations, there is no one left to push it.

Sometimes a product is even tainted by the personality of its champions. A number of years back a company wanted to develop a dramatically new approach to bicycle saddle design because their old design was being priced out of the market. They hired an "idea" man. He was that—but he was also an arrogant screwball. Within weeks he had alienated everyone in the factory. He developed the product they sought—a good design, attractive in appearance, embodying a fraction of the number of parts and production operations of the previous model. Sales potential was extremely high and profits were attractive. But the idea was never even considered: it was "that guy's" idea.

Through most of these runs a familiar theme: the sales push either starts too soon or never starts at all. No planned effort is made to give a well-timed introduction and intensive sales effort for the first two or three years. The end result, a few years later, is a neglected product. They make marvelous opportunities for latter-day heroes who will do a proper job of sales development.

WAS IT EVER WORTHWHILE?

Do a thorough market analysis to learn the industry sales volume, the penetration rate achieved, and the historical patterns over the past decade. Then use the industry history to forecast sales for 5 and 10 years ahead. Of course, these are "guesstimates," but if you take 10 years of industry sales history and simply draw a straight line into the future, it gives you some idea as to whether the market is going up or is drifting down.

Study the history and financial success of competitors. Do they all have similar or established designs or have they modernized their products and left your firm's product behind? Redesign activity is a clue; unchanged designs either mean that competition feel the market has no future—or that they are wrong too. After reflection, is the market still attractive, still worth going after?

If yes, then take a long cold look at the product itself. Read complaint reports and sales correspondence concerning the product; talk to the salesmen to get their experience with customers. Be certain that the product has been reasonably trouble-free, and that it compares well with competition. The objective is to be absolutely certain that the product does not need redesign—this opens a different Pandora's box.

If everybody agrees that the product is excellent, you may not be digging deeply enough. Perhaps a more useful approach is to ask the sales people, "How *can* the design be improved?" If this produces any worthwhile ideas, shelve the product, since if it can be significantly improved, this should definitely be done before starting serious market development.

Often you will find an abbreviated product line—where a product is made in a narrower range of sizes than competitors'. An abbreviated product line is a millstone. It is extremely difficult to put major sales pressure behind a product when the competition offers the same thing in a greater array of sizes or shapes. Such a product was incompletely developed; stay away from it.

PLANNING THE SALVAGE JOB

The likelihood of finding a neglected product, completely free of blemishes and defects, and just waiting for you, is almost nil. A feel for the history of the product is more important than the statistics of that history. Nonetheless, it is wise to ascertain some current data:

Return on investment in facilities
Return on inventory investment
Inventory turnover
Market penetration
Productivity (sales dollars/productive employee) compared with competition
Success ratio of bids and major sales presentations
Repeat sales vs. first-time customers

Delivery—promised, actual, and compared with competition
Percent of customer rejections, by both defective and nondefective units
Days required to process quotations—maximum, minimum, and average
Sales lost because of stock outs
Adherence of product to specifications—quality control
Amount of salvage and rework
Production capacity of present facilities

At the very least, a long hard look must be taken at inventories, production methods, and production capacity. This is vital—otherwise the product will go into a poor delivery situation if sales mount faster than the factory can handle.

There is no point in getting new customers when no customer will repeat his purchases if he gets badly burned on delivery. Delivery is all important—more important than price. The only thing which might loom more important is quality control—not quality of the design—simply quality control. Pure salesmanship can override pricing differentials, a high level of salesmanship might do something to combat poor delivery, but when the customer has finally opened the box, if all he finds is garbage—you will never see him again. Quality control should go without saying—you cannot make a *bad* product and survive. But assuming that quality is what it should be, delivery reigns king. If delivery is maintained, all else becomes possible. But if delivery is neglected, you are forced along an endless line of new customers, seeking replacements for the old ones.

At this stage of the game the question of production capacity can be handled informally—ask people, "What is our capacity per month of X product?" Make it plain that you are considering proposing a major sales push. Ask everybody who might know or have an experienced opinion—foremen, supervisors, vice presidents, everybody you can think of. Add their opinions up and divide by the number of men. If production capacity is not great enough to accommodate a major sales increase, life can become complicated and this product may be a poor selection. However, if the capacity is 4 or 5 times the sales volume—if it exceeds that which can be achieved simply by adding a second or third shift—you are on safe ground. With proper handling, you can convince management to increase capacity if you reach the present ceiling.

If shipping and packaging are important aspects of the product, they may become trouble spots. Since these procedures are intimately tied to the sales volume, you may need major revisions if sales go up. Talk with the man in charge of packaging and shipping and go over your tentative thinking with him. Warn him to work up plans for packaging and shipping requirements for various sales levels. Nothing need be done yet, but he should be prepared to see sales mount and have his plans ready.

Meet with the people who manage the inventory. Financial people keep a very close eye on their inventory investment. Liquid capital is tied up in only three major areas: accounts receivable, in-process inventory, and finished-goods inventory. Of these, the last two are the easiest to control. For this reason, inventory of finished goods is usually the minimum necessary for the sales volume. Where sales are steady and predictable, this is good management. But the reorder points, reorder quantity, and lead time for the production runs will not be adequate if sales volume increases rapidly.

Furthermore, these values are usually reviewed infrequently—twice a year, or even annually. A sharp increase in sales will not be detected rapidly enough to permit adjusting the numbers upward. If the inventory falls behind the rising sales volume, delivery slows and production winds up working directly against customer orders, rather than restocking the shelves. Chaos can result, with factory costs soaring because of short runs and too many setups, restock orders held up while customer orders are pushed, etc.

Therefore, it is vital that inventory control people be brought into early conversations. The easiest way is to assume sales increases of certain levels—25%, 50%, 100%, 500%—and ask the inventory-control people to draw up tentative inventory minimums and reorder quantities for these sales volumes. Further, suggest that they plan constant reviews so that they can move fast when sales start up.

Planning the salvage job will ultimately wind up in a proposal to management. It will include many things, but nothing is more important than consideration of the production and inventory factors which determine your ability to deliver the product after it is sold.

GETTING ACQUAINTED WITH THE SALES DEPARTMENT

Selling is the interface between your company and the customers—a business of people and personalities, completely unlike the people/equipment/machinery associations within the company. Typically, the sales department is long on personal feelings, guesses, hunches, optimism and frustration—and often very short on analysis, objectivity, forecasts, and coherent planning. The sales department's accomplishments are concrete (measured by a very accurate yardstick—dollars) but next week, next month, next year—all are usually vague and nebulous bridges to cross as they arrive.

The sales department accomplishes its monthly sales goals by selling the easiest products to the easiest customers. This probably occupies 75% or more of their efforts. Then comes selling the tougher products to these easiest customers, which occupies another 10% or so. Then (or perhaps) comes selling the easier products to the tough customers. There never seems to be any time at all for selling the tough products to the tough customers. By definition, a neglected product is one which has gotten lost in this shuffle; at this stage, the neglected product is definitely a "tough product." Yet the sales manager is under constant pressure to build sales—plus being the kind of man he is, he will want to. So every product that offers potential sales is welcome—if worthwhile.

The sales manager will be completely familiar with the neglected product which you selected and with your interest in it. Go over your tentative plans with him, covering the conversations you have had with production, packaging, inventory, and finance people. Convince him that the forces which determine availability, pricing and delivery of the product can be gathered to make it salable in volume.

Once he is assured that sales retardants can be eliminated, he should be willing to work with you in drafting a complete sales program for the product. It requires deliberate charting of future sales, and then making the necessary plans to make certain that these predictions come true. This planning is long term—two or three years minimum, preferably 5 years or longer. Part of it means drawing up a specific program for reintroducing the product to the salesmen, getting them to be interested and optimistic, then introducing the product to the distributors—all before sales even get started.

In most cases the new-product manager will actually draft this sales program himself. The average sales manager simply does not think in such calculated, premeditated terms. In some cases, the program will have to be sold to the sales manager piecemeal, tactfully, and probably over a period of time. The one point which the new-product manager must sell convincingly is that routine sales efforts will accomplish little. You cannot simply add the product back into the line and let it paddle itself. Nor can you hold a sales meeting, get everybody stirred up, and then walk away and forget it. If you do, the salesmen will too. Preplanning is essential.

The important thing is to make certain that the sales manager is sold on both the product and the plan. His lack of interest is fatal, his resistance doubly so. Without him, the project can never get off the ground at all. But the purpose of these preliminary conversations is to bring agreement. By now the sales manager has no major objection to the product—although he may have some natural reservations concerning it. Remember, he has already been burned once on the product.

With the sales manager interested and sympathetic, drafting the sales plan poses no major problem. Sales and promotion go hand-in-hand; the sales program must include plans for advertising and sales promotion. Advertising is presented in the next section, but at this point it should be made clear that while the new-product manager makes plans with both the sales manager and the advertising manager, the completed sales program is a blend of the two—sales activity and promotion to back it up.

To organize a sales program, start by specifying the sales volume intended at the end of years 1, 2, 3, etc. Then list the larger known prospects among present customers. Assign conservative dollar sales goals to each one. Then juggle them to account for at least half of each year's sales goals. If you do not have enough identified prospects among present customers, add those whom you do not now sell—but keep them out of the first-year list. And if you do not have enough prospects at all, then do more work in tracking down larger firms in the SIC groups which represent your market. This is work—but makes sales planning a simple, straightforward process. And with the details down on paper, it is easy to visualize the work involved in getting the sales needed.

With the annual sales levels agreed upon, and the target prospects pinned down, then decide upon the things that must be done before sales can begin:

1. Announcement to the sales force.
2. Schedule the sales meeting.
3. At the meeting, reintroduction of the product to the salesmen; education, assignment of prospects, etc.
4. Presentation to the distributors.

The sales meeting plan takes some thinking and conversation. A sales meeting is merely an opportunity to gather the salesmen together in one place and make an organized presentation to them This is convenient, gets the message to the entire sales force at one time, irons out problems, lets technical people get involved—and the salesmen catch fire from each other.

There will be leaders in a group of salesmen, the same as there are leaders in any group of men. If you can reach these key men and get them enthusiastic about the product, then the other salesmen will follow. Cheat if necessary—talk with the key men beforehand, answer their questions, and get them on your side. A really productive sales meeting involves a great deal of salesmanship, some showmanship, and a certain amount of razzle-dazzle. If the sales manager and the new-product manager cannot do this, then they should find someone who makes a good M.C.

After the presentation to the salesmen come presentations to the distributors. If these number in the scores or hundreds, the job becomes a major problem. The new-product manager should expect to carry the first few and it may be best if he expects to hold the sales presentations to all the leading distributors. It is usually impractical to gather a large number of distributors together in one place. Distributor executives, yes—but not distributor salesmen, and they are the men you must reach.

List the most significant 10 or 20 distributors and plan on making individual sales presentations to them. Have the salesman who covers the territory attend and help—not so much to actually assist, but so that he knows what is going on—since he will be expected to carry the word to the secondary distributors. If necessary, he has to be taught how to do this. As you can see, when the new-product manager becomes involved in a product introduction, he gets extremely involved. All this becomes very time consuming. Nonetheless, the original analysis of the neglected product showed what happens when a major sales program is not mounted. You cannot do without it.

The new-product manager should also plan on joining the salesmen when calling on the first of the prime prospects selected earlier. This may require adroit management of time. Most of the salesmen will want him to help as often as possible—naturally. The new-product manager and the sales manager must determine in advance which prospects are worth having him call upon—and severely limit his sales calls to this list of firms (plus others that might be covered in the same day or on the same trip).

In this way, a complete long-term sales program is drawn up. Forecast the expenditure of time by the sales department and the new-product department and the costs involved. The program must represent the agreed-upon thinking of the sales manager and the new-product manager. Once it is finished to their satisfaction, the biggest planning hump is over.

GETTING ACQUAINTED WITH THE ADVERTISING DEPARTMENT

Compared with the sales department, this is both easier and tougher. Easier, because with the sales manager sold, the advertising manager usually comes automatically. Tougher because advertising a new product—promoting for a major sales increase— requires a completely different advertising concept than is usual in the routine promotion of established products. There is a vast array of promotion tools, each capable of almost infinite variation. Few advertising managers are familiar with them all. Nonetheless, the new-product manager must know enough to evaluate the suitability of the advertising manager's thinking.

If you can, guide him to get a good program planned. If he will not be guided, you must develop your own. If so, do it in rough form and discuss it with the advertising manager. There is a lot of work in drafting a program. He may accept someone else's work and adopt it with only insignificant changes. This is the objective. However, if the advertising manager balks, or is completely immersed in buying printed forms and looking for inconsistencies in magazine circulation statements, then don't worry about it. Develop the promotion program you need, sell it to the sales manager, and let the chips fall where they may.

Promotional tools are discussed in greater detail in Chapter 15. At this point all that is necessary is to develop the program in sufficient detail so that a budget can be estimated. For a program to introduce a new product and keep heavy pressure behind it for the first few years, the new-product manager should consider a number of different devices.

Magazine Space Advertising—

For most companies, this represents the bulk of their advertising activities. It becomes thoughtless routine and is often completely useless for introducing a new product. For rapid sales gains, you need more than pretty pictures—you need advertisements that work. Stay away from "arty" or "clever" ads. An eye-catching photo of the product, a meaningful headline, supplementary drawings where applicable, solid factual copy with customer benefits—and feature the literature. Legitimate, worthwhile inquiries are the objective. After screening, they becomes sales leads—fuel to feed the fire that you will build in the sales department.

Draw up a three-year program. This should be heavy the first two years, and then begin a drift down the third year, heading for routine advertising as the product matures.

The new-product manager should particularly beware of unnecessary creative costs. If he is not personally familiar with advertising costs, it is well worthwhile meeting with a few smaller advertising agencies and getting bids on the creative work. Such an approach may horrify a career advertising manager, but many companies have large prestige advertising agencies and get sloppy about watching costs. Such an agency may be completely unsuitable for the hard work that is involved in introducing a new product. At best, taking bids will show the new-product manager that the creative costs estimated by the advertising manager are reasonable. At worst, it may point out the necessity of selling management on finding a small advertising agency to work with new-product introductions.

Publicity—

The new product probably exists in a number of sizes or versions. Plan on a publicity release (with photograph) on each one of these variations, spaced a month apart. Do not be overly concerned about "newness." The editors of trade magazines will publish releases, regardless of how un-new the product may be, as long as they think their readers will be sufficiently interested to respond. With judicious management you can get a release out every month—and keep it up for a year or more. These are tremendously productive inquiry producers—and there is next to no cost involved. Even if handled by the advertising agency, the complete package including photograph, retouching, copy, duplication, postage, and mailing should be well under $200.

Literature—

Create a new brochure, even if you have one now. You need the look of a new brochure—new photos, new sales features—to interest the salesmen. Since the product is an old one, the present literature probably does not do justice to it anyway. New sales literature is a must for any significant sales program. It should cover four points, in this order:

1. The value to the customer of becoming interested in this *type* of product—push the generic product, as made by the industry. Unless the customer becomes interested in buying this sort of thing, he can never become interested in buying it from you. This is the weak point of most literature.
2. Specific use suggestions—application data, typical case histories, dollar savings through use, before and after, and technical information about use.
3. Having sold the advantages of being interested and how to use the product, sell your brand. Cover exclusive aspects, sales features, and why they are important to the user.
4. How to buy—sizes, shapes, specifications—everything necessary for the customer to select the proper model and make out his purchase requisition.

Where possible, include prices. If the sales program is properly planned, you are unlikely to make any price changes the first year or two. Therefore, date the brochure and put the prices in it. This is much better than a separate price list, since it does not get lost. If the product must be individually quoted, give the customer some feeling for the price range by including typical models or arrangements with their prices.

Most advertising is coy. Prices all too seldom are mentioned, although customers are always interested in the price tag. If interested, he will find out the price eventually. If he is not, maybe he is guessing too high. Either way you win by giving the price.

Before designing your new brochure, survey competition—know what you are up against so that your brochure will look appropriate alongside competitive materials. Do not forget supplemental technical or engineering data, application data, specifications, etc. A series of data sheets is more effective than a single booklet because of their handout and direct mail values.

Get prices from a number of printers, as well as through the advertising department's normal channels. Printing prices vary greatly, as does quality—and agency markups.

Direct Mail—

You will be building a prospect list and a customer list. Direct mail to these names multiplies the number of sales contacts which can be made in a time span. Use it effectively: to actually sell where possible, to get invitations for the salesmen to follow up, and names of longer-term prospects. Direct mail is an extremely potent selling tool, one too often neglected by industry. Get prices from the agency, direct mail houses, and printers.

Trade Shows—

Do not be overly discouraged if the firm is inexperienced in trade-show activity. Many firms with old, established product lines bypass trade shows. But pushing a new product for a major sales increase in a short time is a different kind of ball game. A trade show may be a perfect place to drum up interest, find prospects, get sales leads, even take orders right at the booth. Selling at trade shows is done constantly by experienced exhibitors.

Most worthwhile trade shows are sold out many months in advance. Do not be surprised if your first exhibit cannot be held until the second year. For budgeting, find the cost of booth space, exhibits, and estimate the multitude of accessory costs which are involved in a trade show activity. Do not forget applicable internal time charges for booth personnel.

Presentations—

You will need materials for sales training, sales aids, distributor presentations, etc. Estimate what items might be involved and get tentative costs.

FORECASTING THE ADOLESCENCE PERIOD

Anyone who listens to the weather reports knows that forecasting is an art—not a science. Nonetheless, quite accurate guesses about the future can be made, based upon an analysis of the past. To the forecast figures is added the estimated effect of various activities which will occur. The total is a reasonable projection of the future sales volume.

Start with your analysis of the industry sales of the product over the past 10 years or so. From this, project the next 10 years. This can be done with some assurance by relying upon the sophisticated forecasting done by the government and major research organizations such as McGraw-Hill. For almost every product, you can find some major economic indicator which fits the product's previous 10 years and for which long-term forecasts are available. This indicator may be the number of automobiles sold, production of pig iron, housing, gross national product, etc.—singly or in combination.

Once a good indicator has been identified (and you are satisfied that it has paralleled the industry sales of the product), then see how many forecasts you can find for this indicator. Don't be surprised if the forecasts do not agree. If the sources seem equally experienced, simply add the forecasts and take the average. If no parallel indicator can be found, use the nearest or most logical one and experiment with equations until you obtain a usable fit. Figures 5-1A and 5-1B show a typical problem of this type. You have now predicted the total ocean of opportunity for the product, as made by you and your competitors.

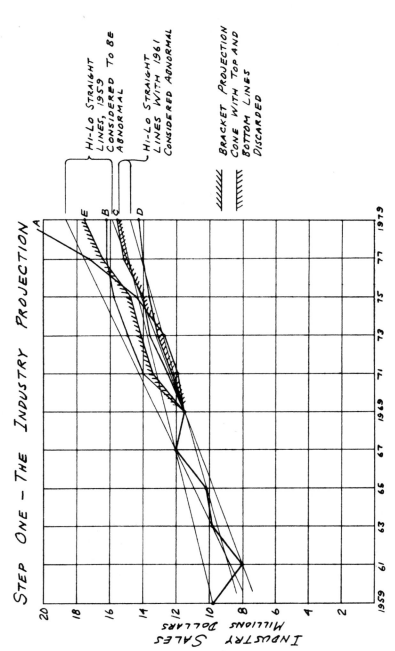

Figure 5-1A

For the product shown, the McGraw-Hill Manufacturing Projection was found to be a useful index for the period 1950 through 1962. However, between 1962 and 1967 the product grew more rapidly than McGraw-Hill, the average annual difference amounting to 6.34%. As shown at A, if this differential is preserved, it leads to unacceptable levels. Therefore, various "decay adjustments" were applied, one of which produced curve B.

Curves C and D are lineal projections, from different base years. The technique consists of selecting a typical time span, determining the average change per year, then extending this same annual change to the future. When different base years are used, the average changes and so does the projection.

Curve E is based upon an inspection of the annual changes, attempting to find cycles or trends, and tailoring the projection by using these adjusted annual rates of change.

Straight line projections frame the high and low years and *suggest* reasonable limits for the forecast.

All the historical data are based upon sales dollars, which ignores (or rather, includes) the effect of inflation, price changes, etc. Thus the projections presume that the future will continue the inflation/price patterns of the past. This is lazy. Much better to take an appropriate base year, convert sales into units, pieces, or tons, and make a double projection—one in dollars and another either in constant dollars or in units. Of course, this requires forecasting the inflation rates for the future.

If you have the time and enjoy variations on a theme, projections can be made in plain forecasting, as in line A, in dollar changes annually (monthly, if you really want to kill time) both in constant or current dollars, by percentage of change (using constant or current dollars)—and then redo everything in units. By the time you finish, you will have a healthy skepticism for any kind of forecast.

86

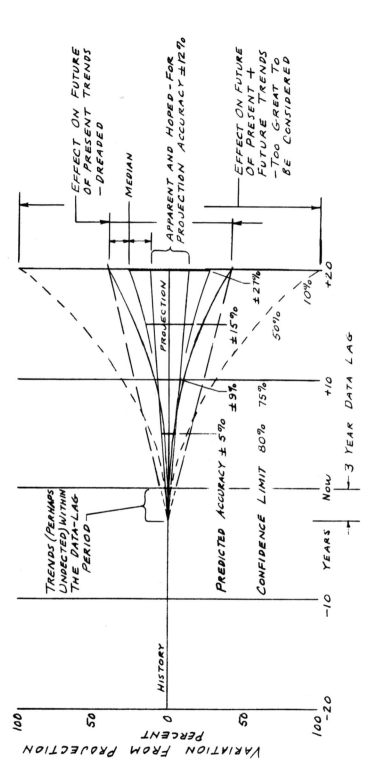

Figure 5-1B

A part of any forecast is a definition of its presumed accuracy—its author's statement of the confidence limits. This is always a neat bit of pomposity, since anyone who is confident of the future has become unhinged.

However, there is, as always, a perfectly rational concept behind the confidence limits. In the previous chart various methods were employed to create a forecast. No two methods will agree so a cone of dispersal is formed. By empirically discarding the two highest and two lowest lines, the projection spread is narrowed. Of course, it is equally logical to discard the bottom and center values and keep the highest. This is only one of the many places where the forecaster must rely upon his judgment.

After narrowing the forecast range, the effect of trends must be anticipated. Data is never current; government figures are always two or more years old and other data is at least a year. Further, *today* cannot really be evaluated until it is *yesterday*. So there are trends, events, forces gathering today which affect the future. Some allowance must be made for them. This is shown as the *effect on the future of present trends*. Then we must also allow for the *effect on the future of future trends* (Figure 5-2c)—whatever they may be. The sum of these events for any period of over ten years usually produces confidence limits of about 10%—that is to say, practically none at all.

87

Then analyze your penetration rate (percent of the total industry) for the last 10 years. If the market is static and your penetration rate has been drifting downward, or has remained about static, then building greater penetration would be very hard work. If the market has been growing and your penetration has been working upward slowly, then gaining greater penetration may not be so difficult.

If a market is growing very rapidly, it may well be expanding faster than the participants can keep up with. You can often spot this by finding a steady influx of new firms through the years. New entrants are seldom attracted to a dying market, but a burgeoning market will be attracting new people constantly.

In meetings with the sales manager, analyze the history of your penetration rate. Not sales volume, but the penetration rate. Based upon the sales program which you developed together, get his estimate of how much your penetration can be increased during the next 3 years. If possible, get him to make a guess 5 years ahead. Using his estimates (and consulting whatever private oracle you prefer) guess far enough out to provide a 10-year forecast. Multiply this 10-year forecast of penetration rate by the 10-year forecast of what your company can hope to accomplish in the next decade, as shown in Figures 5-2A, 5-2B, 5-2C, and 5-2D.

Then go to the financial people in your company with your forecasts, projections, estimated costs for the sales program (and the timing of these costs), inventory investment as required by your sales forecast, production capacity, and the timing when increases in this capacity will be necessary, etc. Work with them in analyzing the data and projecting dollar investments for the company, the timing of these investments, and the profits that can be achieved by the projected sales volume.

The name of the game is money. The entire purpose of promoting the product is to make money. The financial department's forecast of investments and profits is, in the final analysis, all that is really important. Everything else merely goes to show top management how you propose to achieve these profits. So do a careful and thoughtful job when working with the financial department—and convince them of the necessity of doing an equally thoughtful job on their own analysis.

Do not be surprised if this is easier said than done. Accounting and financial people are primarily historians. To be sure, financial management requires looking ahead. However, the financial department is seldom called upon to do its own guessing. It merely takes guesses of other departments—equipment needs, sales forecasts, etc., and translates this into cash flow, inventory investment, accounts-receivable investment, profits remaining, etc. Getting a good, realistic long-term forecast of cash flow and profits can become quite challenging.

In some cases, the financial department will turn a completely deaf ear and you will have to paddle this canoe alone. It is remotely possible to do this. But whenever possible, get the finance people involved in the project. The astute new-product manager will work with other departments so that his final program, as presented to the president, embodies the thinking, opinions, forecasts, and support of all involved department heads. Finance is one of these. They must all be on the team, among those who have contributed to the proposal, if you hope to sell it.

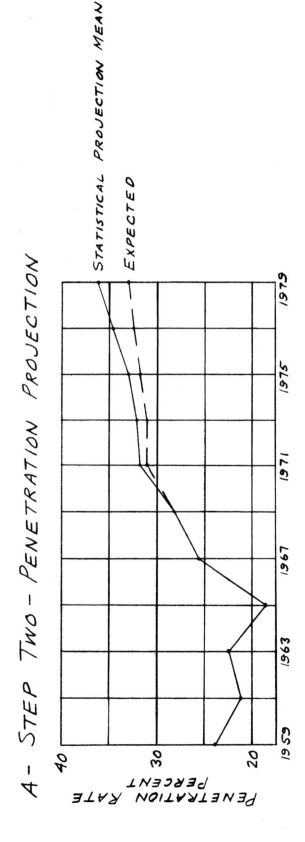

Figure 5-2A

Never attempt a direct projection for the future sales volume for a firm or for a firm's product. There are intervening steps. This is because every firm exists in concert with its competitors, and the sum of their sales can never be greater than the volume of purchases made by customers. No analysis of one company's volume can detect either the industry sales volume or variations in its relationship with competitors. The only logical procedure is to forecast the industry sales volume, then the firm's penetration (share of the market), then multiply the two to obtain the firm's projected sales volume.

As in Figures 5-1A and 5-1B, there are numerous methods for analyzing the data and making the projection, and numerous trends and events that affect the actual numbers. If the projection shows a long-term increase, it is best to apply a gradual decay factor, since it is obvious that penetration growth cannot remain linear for any long period.

The actual cone of dispersal for reasonable projections is actually quite narrow. Competitive pressures eliminate any likelihood of a run-away penetration gain. However, very heavy sales pressure over a number of years can achieve penetration gains so great that others are forced out of the market. Unfortunately, a steadily dropping penetration is the result of the joint efforts of numerous competitors and may be nearly unswervable.

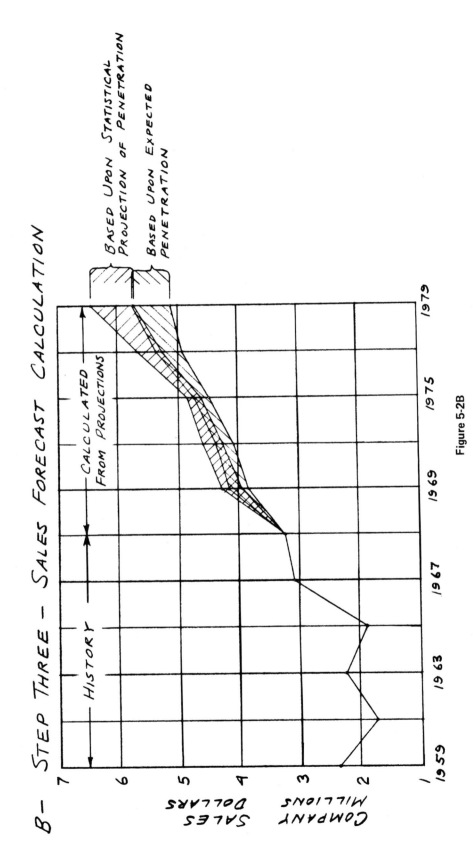

Figure 5-2B

This is the easy part. Just multiply the industry sales volume by the penetration rate. A projection arrived at in this manner can have useful confidence limits, say in the order of 80% for ±5% at 3 years, ±10% at 5 years, ±20% at 10 years. Of course, this requires a relatively straight-line penetration rate and fairly constant relationships between competitors, product lines, prices and delivery, and technology. There are a lot of "ifs" in projections.

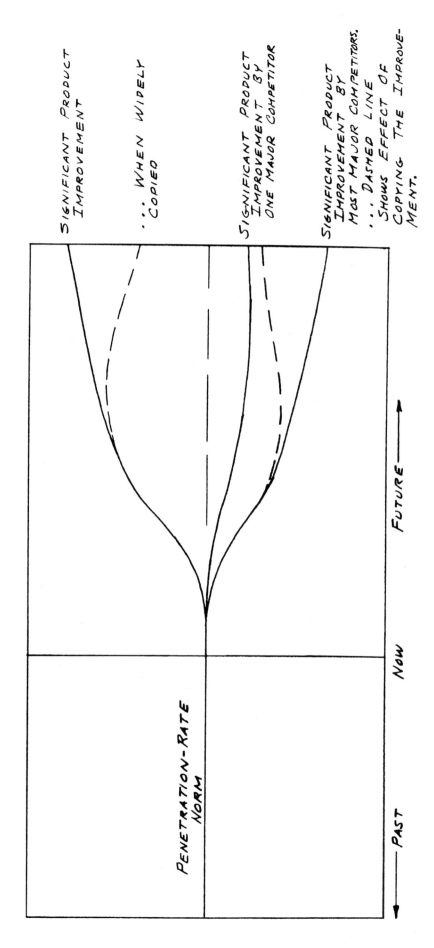

Figure 5-2C

Variables in the status quo affect the future and, as much as possible, must be allowed for in the company's sales forecast. After a projection has been arrived at as shown in Figures 5-1, 5-2A, and 5-2B, it must be adjusted to show any factors that can be predicted as likely/certain to occur. Notice that different occurrences have differing effects, timing, and longevity.

Some variables have long-term accumulative effects. Among the positive ones are better delivery, more aggressive advertising, and significant product improvement (if not excessively copied, although some me-tooism by competition helps convince the customers of the value of the new design). Short-term positive actions include widely-copied product improvements and modest price reductions if not followed by competitors. Obviously, a major price reduction can have a long-range effect, but presupposes competitor indifference or stupidity.

Unfortunately, negatives seem to have more long-term effect than do the positives. This is probably because good moves incur offsetting actions by competitors, while mistakes merely invite increasing competitive pressure and weaken customer loyalty.

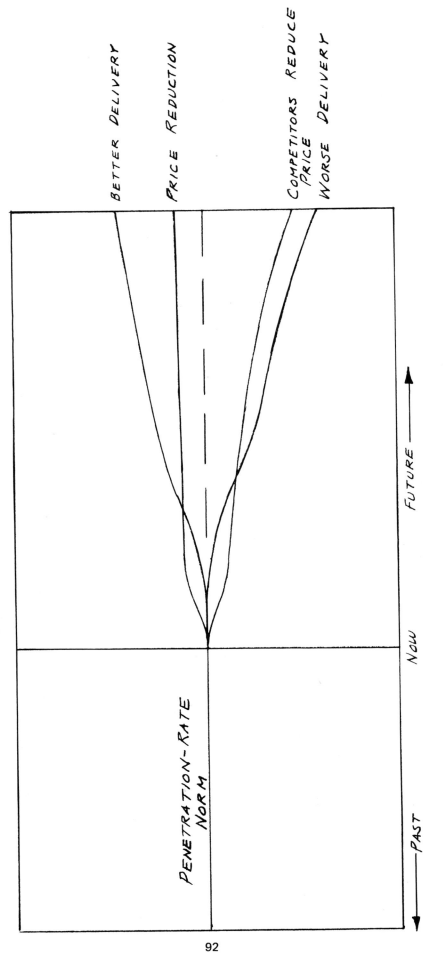

EFFECT OF PRICE & DELIVERY CHANGES

BETTER DELIVERY

PRICE REDUCTION

COMPETITORS REDUCE PRICE

WORSE DELIVERY

PENETRATION-RATE NORM

PAST

NOW

FUTURE

Figure 5-2C (cont.)

92

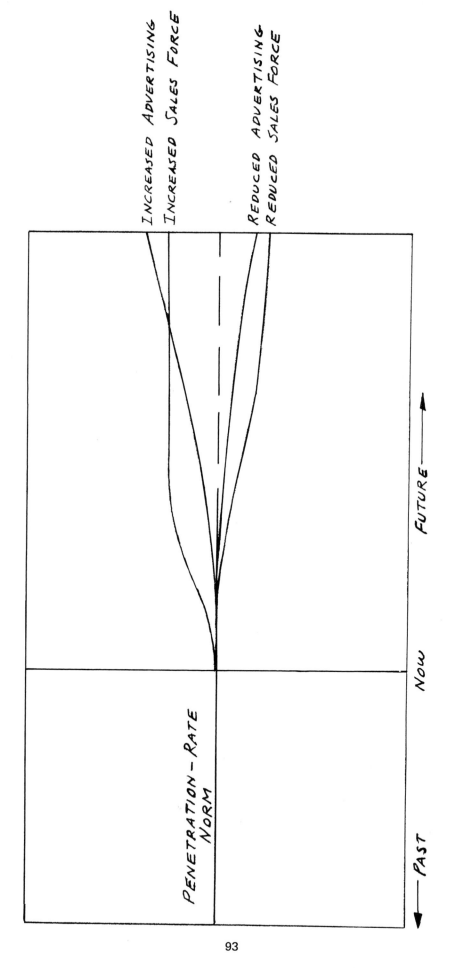

EFFECT OF SALES FORCE & ADVERTISING CHANGES

INCREASED ADVERTISING
INCREASED SALES FORCE

REDUCED ADVERTISING
REDUCED SALES FORCE

PENETRATION-RATE NORM

PAST   NOW   FUTURE

Figure 5-2C (cont.)

93

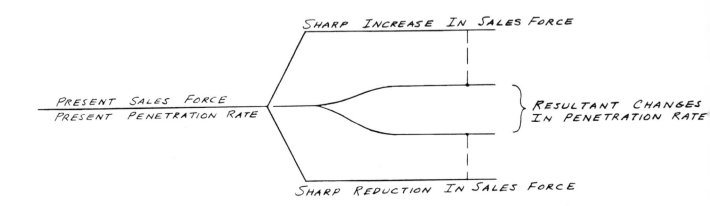

Figure 5-2D

Another variable which affects the future is when a firm—yours or a competitor—changes the size of its sales force by a significant amount (or puts new policies into effect which greatly alter the efficiency of the sales force). Probably the consequences of this change are overestimated; selling tends to reach a market-penetration plateau and, with all competitors in equilibrium, sales volume gradually becomes independent of the number of sales calls. As in all such situations, only movement by someone will break the stalemate. A new product is the ideal move.

PRESENTING THE PROPOSAL

By now you have a great deal of information, a number of estimates, a lot of forecasts, and a surplus of guesses. Make a thorough analysis of all that you have collected, then do some careful thinking. Do not rush. Let it grow cold—do something else for a week while you think about it. There are two questions to be answered:

Does it really look good to you?
Can it be sold to the president as it stands—without major surgery?

Notice that the question is not "Can the new-product manager sell it?" but "Can it be sold?" If the project smells good, arrange all the data, notes, estimates, etc., into some logical progression and draw up a proposal in full detail. Reinforce it heavily with illustrations—anything visual, including engineering drawings, photos of the product, cutaways, charts, graphs, snapshots of the founder's grandparents—anything to break up the text. Plan an illustration at least every third page, preferably every second. When the proposal is typed, have it double-spaced. It means more pages, but makes each one look less formidable. When the tome is finished, put neat covers on it and set it aside.

Then draw up a careful 4-page summary. Keep it to four pages of double-spaced typing—no more. Vital charts and graphs support it. This 4-pager is what management will see; the tome is reinforcement. It will be scanned, flipped through, and its illustrations admired—but nobody will ever read it. Don't expect them to. It serves as your credentials—proof that you did your homework.

You will rise or fall based upon the summary. So do a fussy job—write, rewrite, edit, polish. It is a sales piece, pure and simple. It should be written tightly, concisely, and factually. Do not became flowery. Start out with a brief (one page) sketch of the three and five-year forecasts and of the sales volume and profits that could be achieved. Follow this with your program, using two pages. Step by step, show what each department does and when. Do not miss any department—and be certain to mention each department head by name. This portion of the summary should prove the inevitability of success once the program, as planned, is commenced.

The fourth page is merely a repetition of the first page, using different words. In short, you start with a forecast of what may happen, tell how it could happen, and show the results of the activity described. There is a large element of gamesmanship in the summary—but don't overdo it. This is business, not play. Nonetheless, make certain that each department head is committed. Manufacture concise quotations (three or four words) but do not identify the speaker. If it is about R&D (or whatever), the president can guess the source.

Although the summary is double-spaced, there is room at the bottom of each page for two or three lines of single-spaced footnotes and references to the tome. This adds authenticity to the summary, ties it to the tome, and makes it convenient for the president in the unlikely eventuality that he might want to track down some of the references in the tome itself.

Most important of all, the summary presents the president with two facts—neither of them actually mentioned: 1. The proposal has been thought about, agreed upon, and is supported by all the department heads. 2. The proposal is a concrete, bona fide plan—a logical, organized, step-by-step road map to achieve the forecast goal. The novelty of receiving a well-organized plan may be so great that it will sell itself automatically.

A word about authorship, glory, etc. In any office with three or more people, there is likely to exist some form of "office politics." The author, himself an innocent in such areas, is in no position to suggest ways in which political situations can either be cancelled or used to advantage. However, there are two rather self-evident thoughts: 1. If there are violent political factions within the office, be on the side which the president favors. 2. If a proposal from you to the president would have a poor likelihood of success, select and develop a suitable "front" man. This should be a favorite of the president—or at least someone with an unusually good batting average—who can be relied upon to present your proposal under "good" conditions.

Since political adroitness is a prerequisite of achieving a high station in a corporation where such conditions prevail, it is assumed that the new-product manager is already an old hand at corporate gamesmanship and able to chart his own course.

The presentation is most likely to be verbal, made to the president and a few of the other top executives or to some sort of "planning committee." Most executives feel more comfortable hearing a proposal than reading it. If they have questions they can get the answers. Having the presentation made verbally fleshes it, makes it alive and real. It also adds timeliness—a president is much more likely to respond promptly to a verbal presentation than to a report which arrives with the mail and can be looked at if, as and when he has time.

For the verbal presentation, start with the happy ending. Sell your vision of the company's profits from the successful growth of this product, and where it will stand 3, 5, and 10 years hence. Then describe where the product stands today, and very briefly how it got there (be careful here—there are toes you can step on if you are clumsy). Remember that by virtue of your adroit management and natural leadership, you have all the department heads on your side. Do not undercut them now by implying criticism of their past efforts. This area is quicksand, so pass quickly on to the plan you have drawn up. Go through it step by step, showing the inevitability of success if this master plan is put into effect. Rely heavily on visual aids; blown-up charts of the market opportunities, future penetration rates, sales forecasts, timing of investment, sales to be achieved at end of year 1, year 2, etc. Words alone are not enough. Everyone will quickly tire of looking at you—they will need other things to look at also. Use showmanship—not much, just enough to interest your primary audience, to stir his ambition, to challenge him to leadership.

Unless very large investments are involved (or unless you have severely misjudged the president and his court) the approval should be automatic. A president's job is two-fold: to keep the company going today, and to make certain that it will be going tomorrow. There is no reason why he should disapprove of any program which the majority of his own department heads are supporting. This is what he needs: concerted, organized, deliberate planning by his company. 99.9% of the ideas, proposals, and suggestions which land on his desk are half-baked, not thought through properly—and the president knows this. Much of his time is spent doing the thinking that others did not do and making the plans that others did not think to make. Others make decisions and institute actions, leaving it to the president to forecast the future results. He should welcome a genuine, careful, conscientious, and objective proposal. If he agrees with your analysis and logic, approval will come.

However, do not be surprised if no opportunity is granted to make a verbal presentation. If not, your chances of approval, regardless of the quality of the proposal, are greatly lessened. This does not mean that making a verbal presentation through an intermediary (as mentioned before) is ineffective. A verbal presentation made by anybody will probably do as well, as long as you are present to answer questions and do some steering when necessary. But the president may not take the time to listen to anybody. Perhaps he does not want to formalize the necessity for giving the subject thought, or he feels that he would give too much importance to your proposal by granting a personal audience. This is most unfortunate, and is usually an early sign of a cold winter.

Then you have no recourse except to send the proposal up to him through the chain of command or by the office mail. A last hope might be to try for permission to personally deliver the proposal to the president's desk. Not to his secretary—to him. Once you get into his office, he can scan the four-page summary in a minute or two. Some presidents are wary of formalized meetings and prefer private talks. So you might find yourself making a presentation which, though unscheduled, may be completely satisfactory. But if you cannot reach him, all you can do is send in the proposal and then wait to see if any word comes back.

The president has been perfectly aware of your activity. You have been talking to many people, getting their help, getting quotations, having meetings, asking questions. If after all this expenditure of effort, he is unwilling to even listen to its fruits, then he is unlikely to have any significant interest in new-product development. And you should have gotten to know him better before wasting your energy.

THE DECISION

Decisions come in four varieties: 20% are sharp clear-cut "yes," 10% are sharp clear-cut "no," and the remainder are "yes, but" or "no, but."

Starting with the simplest type of decision, a straightforward "no," the obvious next step is to shove the proposal in the nearest waste basket, lick your wounds, and start over. But if you can, discuss the matter with top-management members. Not to try for a rematch, but to understand the decision. The project looked attractive to you. Since the project did not look attractive to top management, then you are out of phase, and in trouble. To come anywhere near reasonable effectiveness, you should be able to predict the president's reaction with some certainty. If you cannot do this, you cannot hope to accomplish anything worthwhile.

The "no" decision may have a time- or event coupled factor. That is, it may be, "Not now but perhaps after Joe retires, or we finish the expansion," etc. These brush-offs are found in endless variety. However, occasionally one is genuine. In this case, you can file the proposal away and then bring it out for reappraisal at the appropriate time. If over six months pass before the condition is fulfilled, the data will need to be updated before the presentation.

Any answer other than a pure "yes" or a pure "no" leaves everyone up in the air. You have received neither approval nor disapproval, permission to go nor to stop, to proceed nor to abandon it. What you do with the decision is usually left up to you. Sometimes the president will avoid a decision—leaving it squarely in the hands of the new-product manager. Perhaps he wants to see what will happen. This can be rationalized as giving you a free hand to develop your talents and demonstrate your capabilities—or as giving you enough rope to hang yourself. It depends on how you view things.

If you decide to proceed, you are assuming an awesome responsibility with little chance of success, since top management will not support you if you run into resistance from somewhere else in the organization. Further, new-product development means spending money. Can you do it without a formal authorization? Of course, if you succeed, you are a hero. But if you fail, you will either be on the street or shifted to a flunky position.

In the author's experience, if one is to sin then let it be a sin of commission, rather than omission. It is much more enjoyable regretting having done something than regretting not having done something. If you proceed you may have a 50-50 chance of winning. But if you stand pat, your chance of winning is essentially zero.

A clear "yes" is a license to proceed. In fact, it is such a carte-blanche license that you'd better get it in writing. You don't need a contract—a simple one-line note signed by the president will suffice. But since even presidents tend to have poor memories, having the "yes" in writing is a good idea.

CARRYING THE BALL

Once the proposal has been approved by the president, it is a simple matter to put it into effect. The proposal embodies the action plan, all worked out in advance. All eventualities have been foreseen (hopefully), lead time and cost for each step has been agreed upon, and the project should proceed in an orderly manner, step by step. The president, by approving the program, has approved the investments that are required. Nothing holds you back—except the commonest deterrent of all: insufficient desire.

The approval is followed by a let down. Actually starting the project seems anticlimactic. So commence with a quiet desk operation—timing. Take a calendar and organize schedule dates into the master plan. Break the plan and schedule up into sections, have it duplicated, and the appropriate portions provided for each department head involved. Each should also receive his budget, deadlines, and a summary of the activities and timing of departments which affect his operations, plus those which precede and follow him. It is your job to coax the project through each department in turn. It is a job of management, pure and simple, with only hints of con-man, Pied Piper, and slave driver. In any case, the opportunity to run the project was solicited. You now have the opportunity, and it is up to you to perform. Your own plan points the way.

By now, it should be obvious why it was urged that the neophyte new-product manager start by resuscitating an existing product. It is much easier, faster, less traumatic, and less risky financially to bring along a neglected product than it is to start from scratch. Everybody involved is familiar with the product—this in itself is a great help. The estimates and forecasts are much more accurate than with an unknown product. The new-product manager gets into his first project without the necessity of working with the entire company. To a large degree, production, tooling, engineering, R&D, and some other departments are excluded. They do get involved, but only to a minor degree and the involvement is relatively simple. Since a new-product manager frequently has little experience in these areas (alas), the first project gets his feet wet with no danger of his drowning.

You deal with a smaller segment of the company: fewer people to coordinate, fewer people to work with, fewer people to get acquainted with, and fewer places to have trouble. The new-product operation can start with a small staff—one man if necessary. Overhead is next to nothing and the manager has a chance to prove what he can do before his operation and his overhead become conspicuously expensive.

Presented from the standpoint of immediate profit returns to the company, escalating an existing product is ideal. The sales people need little education, some customers already exist, there is enough familiarity with the product to know precisely where the major prospects are, and many of the distributors will already be favorably inclined toward the new product.

In every possible way, by reviving a neglected product you have stacked the cards in your favor. Now all that is needed is to play your hand judiciously—and the 19:1 odds against you shift to 99:100 for you. This is profitable new product development, with the emphasis on *profitable.*

Ideas Worth Exploring—No. 4

BOOKS

Description: Any objective and accurate book published concerning the types of products which the firm manufactures, the types of work in which the products are used, or of general interest to the market served. The range could include purely technical books, general reference or how-to books, and ones useful in training employees.

Marketing Comments: One of the perennial problems in selling industrial products is the ignorance of the customer. An extremely large percentage of selling is purely education—helping the customer understand how he can profitably employ the type of product the firm sells, helping design his application or selecting the correct product for his requirement, and then helping him use and service the product after he buys it. The majority of industrial service calls—whether the product is a machine, tool, component, supply, etc.—are caused by the user's lack of familiarity with the product involved. This lack of know-how is expensive to both buyer and seller.

If the seller exposed his customers to worthwhile useful books, they could increase their knowledge, with a corresponding increase in their efficiency and a reduction of their costs.

There are a number of trade journals which contain pertinent and valuable information for every man—regardless of his industry or job function. Unfortunately, magazines offer a transient sort of information—in spite of old-issue collections and the indexes which a few leading magazines offer, the magazine is for "now" reading—useful only when the magazine is in hand. When a problem (or curiosity) arises, it is usually not practical to search for the answer in magazines—that is what books are for.

But most book stores do not carry any significant inventory of technical or trade books. Even if they did, the average engineer, purchasing agent, methods man, or production supervisor seldom has the opportunity to go into a bookstore; and when he is there, his mind is not on work. The end result is that most company bookcases are notable for their profusion of catalogs and their paucity of books. Too few people in industry are exposed to the wealth of extremely useful information available in books, and remain ill-informed in many areas where knowledge would be profitable.

A company selling almost any kind of product or service would find its selling and service jobs easier if the customers were better informed. Therefore, it appears logical that companies might find it profitable to explore the practicality of locating a list of books appropriate to their market and their products and offering these as a standard part of their line. The discount on books averages around 40%. This margin is adequate to make the selling of books at least a marginally profitable operation, often including the distributor discounts involved.

The profit from book sales is secondary, of course—the object is to use book sales to create more knowledgeable customers for the firm's other products.

This unexplored area deserves attention. The volume of books which could be moved by a major company, through distributors and thousands of customers, would be substantial. Such a campaign should create better-advised customers who would then be better able to more widely apply (and more correctly apply) the company's products.

An idea well worth exploring.

Chapter 6

Maximizing "New" New-Product Success

> ... more complex, more expensive, and more risky than resurrecting a faltering product, is the development of a product to compete with essentially similar ones now made by others. This is the most popular form of new product—when a firm surveys various product/market mixes, finds one which appears to welcome a new contender, and jumps in. However, because of the host of new entries each year, here is also found the largest number of flops. This chapter shows how to look before you leap—then how to do so with maximum certainty.

WHAT DOES "NEW" MEAN?

Near the end of Chapter 4, three classes of new products were suggested. There is the *old* new product, one which is already in the firm's line but which has been neglected, never brought to full realization of its market potential—although the product suffers from no other defects of design or usefulness. The second is the *new* new product—not new to the industry, but new to the firm. It could also be an existing product which requires extensive re-engineering, either to correct functional defects or to update it. These products are developed (or redeveloped) to compete with existing ones made by other firms. The third is the new-idea product, the original laboratory breakthrough—a product which is unlike any product sold before.

This chapter considers the middle one—the product which is not new to the world but is new to your firm, or which exists but requires extensive redesign.

The *new* new product offers many benefits over the new idea, since the product already exists and minimum engineering is necessary—you have something to copy. If specific engineering skills are necessary, you can always hire an experienced man away from one of the competitors or major users. Marketing and technical data is available. Most market and engineering research can be performed at the library. Customers already exist and are known; the selling job consists of shifting them from their present supplier to your firm. Minimal salesman and distributor training is necessary since presumably the product considered is one already known to the distribution channels.

For these many reasons, the *new* new product is the most popular of all. Successes in new-product marketing are most likely to be found in this type. Actually, the *old* new product considered in the previous chapter is the most successful—but since it is not usually considered a new product, it does not show up in the statistics. It offers the greatest chance for profit and the least risk. The *new* new product, covered in this chapter, is the second-best choice.

MARKETING FOR FUN AND PROFIT

There are two directions in which to search for likely products. The commonest approach is to find a product quite similar to others now being made, where minimum new engineering or production experience is necessary. Unfortunately, this often carries the firm into a new market, with disastrous results. For example, a major manufacturer of electronic acoustical instrumentation had a broad line, sold primarily to research laboratories and instrumentation manufacturers. Among the products was a set of instruments used by hearing-aid manufacturers for determining the acoustical profile of hearing-aid units. The firm decided to develop a simplified version for sale to the individual hearing-aid dealer. In spite of a major investment in development and promotion, the product was a complete flop. The salesmen, busy selling instrument systems to steady customers, with the value of most sales running into "kilobucks," could not become interested in one which sold for less than $2,000, was a one-shot sale, and required chasing after a large number of small, cautious, and often technically uninformed retail dealers of hearing aids. The result was zero—as is usually the case when engineering or production considerations dictate the direction of new-product development.

The intelligent approach is to find a product which can be manufactured on existing facilities, although it may be substantially different from existing product lines. However, it should be within the experience (or readily trainable knowledge area) of the sales force; and salable through the same distributors, and to the same customers. An example might be a firm now making tool-room lathes and shapers, which decides to offer a line of tool-room surface grinders. This will probably be successful because it is based on sales convenience, even if gained at the expense of engineering and production inconvenience. The engineering and production problems, once solved, are over with. But a selling problem may never really be solved. The only way the instrumentation manufacturer could ever have succeeded would have been to establish a completely separate sales organization for that one product. Only the very largest firms are able to do this successfully—and most of them have sufficient marketing orientation to avoid the problem. Your best chance of success is in developing new products for existing customers and prospects. New markets can be added, but the more they overlap with existing markets, the better.

Based upon your analysis of the company's growth directions, list the markets of greatest interest, and potentially interesting products which those markets now buy from other companies. Note particularly those which are in or near the existing product line, sell for roughly the same amount of money, and fit within the scope of the salesmen's ability to become expert with minimal training. Further, sort out those which can be sold through the existing distribution channels.

For example, if your firm now makes plastic plating tanks and barrels, the addition of corrosion-proof blowers is practical. Photo-lab equipment would be out because it is a different market with different customers and the salesmen need to learn too much. Anodes, anode bags and filter elements would be worse yet. These are disposable items; the dollar volume per sale is too low and the salesmen would not be interested. You would be entering a completely new type of selling, trying to move low-dollar, repeat-sale items with salesmen who are experts in pushing relatively expensive capital equipment. This is done from time to time—equipment makers selling the perishable items involved with the equipment—but except for those firms who started years ago, you seldom find a successful example. And these people are wide open to aggressive competition—indeed, practically invite it.

These suggested limitations probably sound conservative. They are meant to be. Industry tends strongly to make flamboyant new-product moves in a hyper-conservative way. This is backwards—if you want to make money, make conservative moves in a flamboyant manner.

Look at your sales force—they are experts at what? Production woodworking machinery, packaging delicate products, moving heavy bulk goods? Define the areas where your sales force has truly competent know-how—then add the wider band of areas which would be relatively easy for them to learn. Identify and discard those portions of this wide band which are outside the markets where you are now established. Usually a well-defined pathway becomes apparent.

Now list the products which exist in this area of sales expertise and near-expertise. For instance, if you now make strapping wire and associated tools, the list might include tapes, glues, sealing machines, wire-bound crates, disposable pallets, etc. Look for new-product ideas here, close to home markets. By playing them against your factory, you can sort out and discard those which involve extreme manufacturing changes—but as long as you keep your new product within the framework of what the sales department can sell you are on safe ground. A way for visualizing and ranking various products is shown in Figure 6-1.

Talk to the salesmen, your distributors, and some of the customers. Search out the trade journals, go to trade shows—dig, ask, read, search, and make lists. Once you have a lengthy list of likely products, sift them. Save two or three which fit your distribution channels, your salesmen's expressed interest, and your present production facilities. These are your best prospective products.

RANKING BY DIFFICULTY

Firm now makes electric motors, ¼–2 HP

Marketing & Distribution (weight 2X)

1. flange-mounted motors, user market
2. motors larger than 2 HP
3. motor mounts
4. electric clutch/brake units
5. adjustable-speed drives
6. motors under ¼ HP
7. flange-mounted motors, oem market
8. speed reducers
9. d-c motors
10. shaft couplings
11. chain drives
12. V-belt drives

Sales (weight 3X)

1. motor mounts
2. flange-mounted motors, user market
3. shaft couplings
4. motors larger than 2 HP
5. motors under ¼HP
6. V-belt drives
7. adjustable-speed drives
8. chain drives
9. electric clutch/brake units
10. flange-mounted motors, oem market
11. d-c motors
12. speed reducers

Production (weight 1X)

1. flange-mounted motors, oem market
2. flange-mounted motors, user market
3. motors larger than 2 HP
4. electric clutch/brake units
5. motor mounts
6. shaft couplings
7. speed reducers
8. d-c motors
9. V-belt drives
10. motors under ¼ HP
11. adjustable-speed drives
12. chain drives

Engineering and Design (weight 2X)

1. flange-mounted motors, user market
2. flange-mounted motors, oem market
3. motor mounts
4. shaft couplings
5. motors larger than 2 HP
6. adjustable-speed drives
7. speed reducers
8. motors under ¼ HP
9. electric clutch/brake units
10. d-c motors
11. chain drives
12. V-belt drives

Typical Scores:
Electric clutch/brake units—26 unweighted, 57 weighted
Flange-mounted motors, oem—20 unweighted, 49 weighted
Flange-mounted motors, user–6 unweighted, 12 weighted

104

Figure 6-1

A potential new product will represent different levels of compatibility for different departments. This is an easy way to visualize the average level of difficulty. The firm shown makes electric AC motors, in the size range of 1/4–2hp. Obviously, the easiest and most compatible step is to widen the size range somewhat.

But, for a list of new products, discuss them with the department heads and make a list for each department, with the products arranged in order of increasing difficulty. The ranking for each department must be weighted, since a production difficulty does not carry as much long-term significance as a sales problem.

Discuss the two or three products with *thinking* department heads. Get their opinions, comments, and suggestions. If one of the products gets knocked out of the hat, replace it with another from your list. The idea is to wind up with two or three potentially interesting products. After analysis, you will refine this to one.

PRELIMINARY ANALYSIS

For each of the tentative products, analyze the industrial sales data and economic indicators to make a tentative forecast of the next 10 years. If industry sales are down or up only 20% or so (not growing faster than the inflation rate) drop the product. Keep only those where industry sales are rising—the faster the better.

Using one of the popular purchasing directories *(Thomas Register, MacRae's Blue Book, Conover-Mast),* make a list of the present firms making the product. From the local library obtain old directories and make a similar list for as far back in the 10 years as you can reach. Compare the two lists to see how many companies have entered the arena and how many have dropped out. If there is a steady influx of new firms, this is a good sign. A fast-growing field attracts new business because the established suppliers are often not able to keep up with it.

Analyze the profit of the leading makers. If they have slim profits yet the industry continues to attract new companies, this is not necessarily a paradox. New manufacturers usually employ the latest equipment, methods and technology while old-time established firms are often unable or unwilling to keep their operations up to date. They wind up with a high-volume but profitless product while the Johnny-come-latelys take off all the cream. This has happened, for instance, in carbide cutting tools. Newer firms making extensive use of EDM, EDG, ECG, and other new methods of working with carbide, are making money while established companies, reluctant to discard familiar methods, are losing their shirts.

Calculate the dollar sales volume per industry employee. Then use your data on the number of employees for the larger competitors to figure their sales—then compare it with sales volume as found through other sources. If the correlation is good, repeat for 5 or 10 years ago. This gives changes in penetration rate for the leading makers. In an ideal market, the penetration rate of the leading makers is drifting downward, the gap being filled by newer companies.

From conversations with salesmen, distributors, and customers (or via market research) find out the present delivery situation. Particularly, learn the difference between the older firms and the new firms. Then analyze this delivery in terms of the theoretical ideal: would the customers be best served if this product were shipped off-shelf? Is two weeks reasonable? Six, eight weeks, three months? Compare this with the industry performance. There are three signals emitted by a genuine market opportunity:

1. The market is growing at a rate faster than the leaders can maintain, with new firms jumping in to fill the gap between demand and supply.

2. New technology is available and being employed by new firms but is not yet widely utilized by the established firms.

3. The customers have to wait longer for delivery than is theoretically ideal.

Now that you have found and confirmed a few products that offer good development potential, you must learn more about the actual products. It is not enough to say that high-pressure hydraulic valves look good. For every such vague product category there is an endless variety of products now sold, introduced unsuccessfully in the past and dropped, killed off by World War II production controls, etc.

So the next step is to become an expert on the product involved—what engineering concepts are available, what designs and styles exist, which sizes and shapes are made, what ideas can be found in expired patents, etc. This takes digging—a great deal of it.

LOOK FOR FUMBLED BALLS

In the previous chapter, neglected products of your firm were discussed. Here we think of the neglected products of other firms, where a potentially good new product was fouled up. Every market is strewn with them, although they may take some investigation to find. This book contains six such products—Ideas Worth Exploring Nos. 1 through 6. They are not only presented as product ideas but as examples of the sort of opportunities which can be found in any industry.

Recovering the competition's fumbles can produce very attractive new-product ventures. Obviously, you must know more than they do, see opportunity which they overlook—or do an organized, deliberate development job where they muddled along in the usual manner. For example, in the '50s a major machine-tool builder contracted with an inventor to produce his patented machine. They launched the machine with much fanfare and promotion, were immediately successful selling it to automotive plants, and then dropped it. The behind-the-scenes reason was that the company had second thoughts about the royalty percentage and decided to shelve the product until the inventor's patent expired. Unfortunately, a wide-awake competitor had analyzed and was watching the situation. Just a few months before the patent expired, he was in the market place with a Chinese-copy product. The original licensee, caught unprepared and with no plans made for moving fast on D-day, did not have a chance. The end result was that they lost the market by default.

Another example would be the hearing-aid testing device mentioned earlier. This same product, copied and sold by a hearing-aid manufacturer, probably would have been a thundering success. Don't for a second think that your firm is the only one that messes up its new-product development—most firms do. If you are able to do the job right, then opportunities abound. To find these situations, just look for products that were introduced and then seem to have died along the way. Your salesmen, always a group with eyes and ears open, may be able to tell you of a number of them.

Another clue is to look for "orphan" products—a discordant product on the end of a cohesive product line. For instance, a number of machine-tool builders have a cutting-tool line and one cutting-tool firm also makes snowplows! One very large builder of foundry machines also make a vibrating lounging chair. A maker of die sets and press-room equipment has a reamer line. A machine-tool accessory maker also tries to sell equipment to pathology laboratories. A firm with 50 years experience in foundry supplies tried to cash in on the Hoola-Hoop craze! Such "orphan" products are almost invariably unsuccessful. But they may be excellent products for development by the right firm. Often the product line can be purchased outright or arrangements made to sell the product under your own name.

It may sound unfair, but large firms should watch little ones, especially those with only one product. Small companies may have excellent mechanics and come up with products which they cannot sell successfully in volume, just because they do not have the sales/distribution organization required. This is particularly true if the product sells for less than, say, $200. Yet this product, added to a related product line, might readily sell in significant volume.

In summary, look at products which you can sell more readily than the firm now making the product. They may just be ignoring it, may have let costs drift so high that it is no longer profitable for them, perhaps do not realize the potential of their own product, may concentrate their sales effort in other markets, the product may not be compatible with the rest of their line, or require different contacts at the customer's plant, or be of the wrong price category, or perhaps they just do not have the sales organization. Remember the odds—19 out of 20 new products wind up in one of these traps—each one a potential opportunity.

RESURRECTING DEAD IDEAS

Your analysis of the market tells you what is currently being sold and by whom. Now find out what products have died—and might be made to live again—with profit. At the library, make an intensive study of the trade magazines for 10, 20 and 30 years ago. Ideas Worth Exploring Nos. 1, 2, and 3 are typical of product ideas which can be found in this way. Many products, advertised then, are no longer active. Watch for new products which were introduced but never got off the ground. Look for articles concerning likely products, and search the advertisements, particularly the new-product columns. Anything that you can find and which does not now appear in the marketplace (and has not become obsolete) is now a fumbled ball or a dead product.

This is an extremely fruitful source of product ideas so set your nets wide. While you are at it, watch for pertinent technical and case-history articles which might be valuable to you. Have copies made—they are the beginning of your engineering data and may greatly facilitate matters for your own engineers if the product involved passes your screening.

Old catalogs in purchasing-department files are equally fruitful but they are harder to come by. If you have access to a few major purchasing departments who will let you dig around in their files, this can be most rewarding.

Another good source for dead ideas is the *Patent Gazette* of 25 and more years ago. A patent has a 17-year life. Often it takes that long to get a product from the patent stage to market fruition. But if the product is still not marketed, over 5 years after the patent expired, it probably never will be—at least, not by the inventor. The idea was either abandoned or introduced as a new product which contributed to the 19:1 statistics.

By now you know your selected products thoroughly. You know their market history and their market forecasts; who is doing what in the market place and what has gone on before. You have tracked down a number of products with fumbled introductions and abandoned products. You have a long list of sales features, engineering ideas, and design concepts. Further, you know of many expired patents that may have useful ideas.

Now think carefully about what you have learned. Sort out the products, pick one and file the others away. From here on in you work with only the one which you feel is the best. Make certain that your files for this product are truly complete with competitors' literature, price lists, technical and application data, etc. Double check your analyses of the market and the market forecasts. Are they as accurate as you can make them at this stage of the game? Review the designs, and study the sales features and claims by the various manufacturers. Play this against material found from past efforts with the product. Out of this, generate your own engineering and design ideas. A number of people in the company will work with you on them, but you will do better if you know what you want when you start.

DEVELOP VERSUS BUY

There are three ways to acquire a new suit: you can make it yourself, have a tailor make it, or buy one from the pipe rack. The first will be low cost but amateurish, the second high priced but professional (perhaps too much so), and the third is sort of in-between priced, there is no waiting, but it will never quite fit. The same thing holds true of new-product development—you can do it yourself, have someone do it for you, or buy it ready to go.

The new-product manager's job is to conceptualize, plan, and help manage his company's profitable new-product activity. It is myopic to assume that this must all be done internally. Very often a company can save many months of development by buying a firm which already manufactures the product which they want. Frankly, most companies are not bought with this thought in mind—there are many reasons for buying companies (many of them obscure). However, as a general principle, the top management of most firms is interested in acquisition.

The new-product manager has a product which he would like to pursue through the proposal stage; he has done a lot of analysis and a lot of digging. Along the way he formed a long list of small manufacturers of this product, with a comparison of their products, including sales features, specifications, and patents. He has a good idea of their sales volume and profits. He has the same data on "orphan" departments and divisions of major firms. It may well be that one or more of these is purchasable. Under no circumstances should you approach a company that appears to be for sale. However, no harm can come from taking an outside look and preparing a list of such prospects in case management accepts your proposal but would rather buy a going concern than develop the product internally.

There are benefits to buying. First of all, it is the "in" thing to do. It makes everybody feel important; you just step in, pay the asking price, and everything goes great—perhaps. If the purchased company has good management, is large enough to operate as an independent (and is permitted to continue doing so), then things may work out very well indeed. But if the purchased company is much smaller than yours and is to be assimilated, then the purchase may be a great disappointment.

The disadvantages of buying an outside firm include the high price asked today, personnel problems, and the simple fact that companies tend to be much like used cars—if they are for sale there is something wrong with them.

But the biggest problem rotates around what to do with the purchased company once you have it. If you leave it operating as a completely separate unit, it is never a part of your own firm and you may have defeated much of your purpose in buying it. If the intent was to acquire a new product line to be sold by your present salesmen and distributors, then buying a company with its own distribution and running it as a separate entity does not satisfy this requirement. Conversely, if you buy an extremely small company and filter it into your own organization, you run into one simple problem: a little company is different than a big company. By the time you convert a little company to big-company ways of doing things, you are likely to have acquired nothing but some engineering drawings and a few machines.

Ironically, most companies operate backwards after they buy. If they acquire a major firm, they leave it independent, with a complete duplication of their own overhead and sales efforts, when it could be absorbed into the parent, blending overheads, engineering departments, sales forces, machinery, inventories, etc. In this way the original firm becomes larger and there are tangible rewards for having made the purchase. However, when a company buys a miniscule firm it is almost invariably absorbed. By doing so, the buyer eradicates that which he paid for. So if your firm is one of substantial size and you buy an alley shop to acquire its product line—leave it alone, with its present management in charge. In exchange for its product, flexibility, and ingenuity, all you need provide is backstop capital. If you try to absorb it, you displace its head—and without him, you have nothing left.

But in spite of the disadvantages, company acquisition is a popular sport today. So if you are likely to become involved in buying companies, you may as well know how to spot one that is for sale. There are a number of "earmarks":

1. Study the credit ratings and reports on small firms (annual sales under $500,000). Any one with a slow pay record (short of capital) or which is heavily in debt (all the profit goes for dead horses and interest) is probably for sale. The president/owner of such a firm is probably working himself to death and may be delighted to have a rest.

2. Any firm doing less than $3 million annually, where the president is substantially the sole owner and is in his 50's or very early 60's. (If he holds on well past the common retirement age, he plans to take the firm with him when he goes.) If the president's son, brother, or in-law appears as a vice president, wait until he inherits—then the firm will be for sale.

3. In a firm of any size, look for one with a female president. She will be the founder's widow/sister/daughter and her attorney runs the place.

4. In any firm with sales volume of less than $20 million, look for one where the majority of the stock is held by the founder's survivors, none of whom are active in the management of the firm. Find out who their attorney is, and give him a modest retainer to search out firms to buy.

5. In a family-owned corporation of any size, look for one where the president is the son of the founder, provided the father ran the place with an iron hand and the son was in his late 40's or older when his father retired.

6. Any company or division whose present owners have held it over one but less than 3 years. That is long enough to find out what is wrong with it, but not long enough to develop energy for fixing it.

For the purposes of this book, we assume that new-product development will be internal. However, if you bring a proposal to top management you may find the president leaning toward buying rather than doing the work inside. If so, it will do you no harm if you have a list of prospects ready, with the reasons why you think they might be for sale, and what you feel would be a reasonable price to pay for them.

PATENT PROBLEMS?

The product which you selected may have tight coverage by existing patents. You know of most of these, either because the patent numbers were listed in a firm's literature, or were fastened or marked on the product. Occasionally, however, a company will be coy and simply claim that a product is "patented" without giving the patent number involved. This makes sense for them; it makes extra work for you and yet protects their product.

If the patent number is known, look it up in an old *Patent Gazette* to verify its date. If it expires within the year, ignore it. The brief *Gazette* description and illustration may tell you that the patent is of no concern. But if you cannot dismiss it safely, you can buy a copy for 25¢.

If you know that patents exist but do not know their numbers, a lot more work is involved. The best bet is to go to your corporate patent attorney and give him the name of the company or companies involved and tell him you want copies of patents assigned to these firms that involve the product. Be specific—some firms collect patents by the hundred. The search will cost money but it is not an expensive procedure. Once you have the patents in hand, look them over carefully. If you are not too certain about the legalese involved, go over them with your patent attorney. However, if they appear to interfere with what you want to do, do not despair.

It may sound blood-thirsty, but if the company involved is substantially smaller than your firm, ignore the patent and proceed. If the patent holder is your own size or substantially larger (can afford a protracted court fight) then take another tack. Patents are treated more fully in Chapter 10. However, at this point suffice it to say that the average patent probably can be invalidated in court if you do enough research beforehand.

It has been said that there is very little new under the sun—and this is quite true (except possibly for subjects representing the outer fringe of today's technology). A patent is invalid if the idea embodied has been disclosed previously. That means the idea was covered in some earlier patent—issued anywhere in the world, no matter how long ago—or was known and used by someone else in the U.S., or was described in any book or magazine anywhere in the world, no matter how long ago. That includes a lot of territory. So if you are up against a patent that is an obstacle, talk with your patent attorney. Get a quotation on a thorough search of foreign patents (don't bother with the United States; the inventor's attorney would have made a reasonable scrutiny there). Do not confine him to Great Britain and Canada. Include *every* European country. Have him go as far back as is consistent with the dawn of technology for such products. If he pulls a blank, turn to the library.

The most likely place to find something that will blow the patent apart is in old books and magazines. There are many thousands of trade magazines published every year and also many thousands of books. Somewhere in this fantastic mass of paper, the inventor's idea is almost certain to have been published. So pack a lunch box and head for a major library. Be prepared for a long stay—this may take many hours or days of digging. However, most patents can be dethroned in this way.

For instance, during the past 10 years a Clevelander has spent a great deal of money fighting off infringers of a patent on a form of setup block. The idea is attractive, his firm is extremely small, appears to be fair game, and has attracted many copiers. So far, he has spent much more defending his patent than he has made on the product involved—which is unfortunate, since his patent was anticipated in 1948 and 1949 issues of *The Tool Engineer*. A patent on a spade drill, filed in December 1965, was anticipated in an ICS book entitled *Shop Drawings, Measurements, Drilling, and Appliances* and copyrighted in 1914. Ideas Worth Exploring No. 7, now being manufactured under an existing patent, is from another ICS book, this one dated 1901! One manufacturer is advertising a new product, "developed at a cost of over $35,000"—which was sort of wasteful, since the design is described in a 1917 book published by the University of Illinois. So be of stout heart; even if the patent looks impregnable, it probably is not.

GETTING ACQUAINTED WITH ENGINEERING

Engineers are objective, dispassionate seekers after truth and knowledge. They are also often highly opinionated and occasionally quite wrong. Before taking your new product to engineering, give it some serious thought and decide beforehand the features and abilities that you want incorporated. Do not plan on simply taking the best-known competitor and copying his product. First, this is dirty pool. Second, it leaves you with no sales features to discuss. Third, it marks your firm as a number of steps below leadership. Instead, start with the best basic concept which you can find—then improve it. One of the easiest ways is to pick up sales features from other sources and combine them all into one.

At this preproposal stage, you do not want engineering work—you want engineering's ideas on what might be developed, how to accomplish design objectives, what features might be put together, what improvements might be found, how long this engineering will take, and how much it will cost. Before you get into design discussions, analyze the selling prices of competitive products, and determine the price at which you want to sell, the discounts and commissions that are involved, shipping costs, etc. With these numbers in hand, a conversation with finance will tell you the maximum amount of money which is allowable for material cost and factory direct labor.

The product may well be outside the scope of technical knowledge and ability in the engineering department. Therefore, the chief engineer's first task may be to learn about the product. Since this can get touchy, think the problem through well in advance. You have no recourse except to lead this man to become knowledgeable—not to become an expert, but to have a basic understanding of the product. Do not push—if he pretends knowledge that he does not have, he will buttress his ignorance by unshakable opinions. Then you are both on the road to trouble.

Start your discussion in low-powered fashion, and confine it to talking about the engineers who work under him. This is a legitimate problem which also needs examination. If you do not find the necessary experience on the staff, there are only two alternate routes: the first is to educate one or more engineers in the new technologies involved. This usually means building a library and a complete file of magazine articles, so that the engineers can do a self-education job. Buy competitors' products and run tests to get the engineers personally involved with the product. If this is impractical, get them to users' plants so they can examine the products in action.

The second route is to look outside the firm and hire at least one engineer who is skilled and experienced in the product at hand. Doing this has both advantages and disadvantages. Among its disadvantages is the high fixed cost of hiring an engineer for one specific product—and the fact that the people for whom he works may not understand what he is talking about. Further, he will have his own ideas, opinions, and prejudices—and if nobody else knows the product, the firm is at his mercy.

In the engineering planning, two points must be clearly understood and agreed upon:

1. Avoid having the design frozen prematurely. If the project receives management's approval, you want the engineers to retain an open mind so that they can come up with a product which is, if at all possible, superior to anything else on the market. The benefit to sales is self-evident, and as stated before, sales problems are much more lasting than engineering problems.

2. Design details are intimately related to production quantities. Since engineers tend to forget this, it should be agreed that the initial design will be based upon sales volume achievable during the first year. Then, as sales volume accelerates, the design will shift to accommodate the more sophisticated tooling and high-production methods warranted by the increased production. Through the first few years, the design may shift a number of times. Keep the design flexible enough to take advantage of rising production. Most companies do not.

GETTING ACQUAINTED WITH PRODUCTION

You are working on a master plan and proposal that top management undertake development of the product. This development would include design and building of tooling—jigs, fixtures, dies, special machines, etc. However, production would not commence without a final review and approval of top management. Therefore, you are not concerned with getting the product into production—just deciding, with production's help, how to do it.

Production will react to your proposals with either antagonism or resignation. The perennial ideal of production supervision is to make a simple, non-precision, one-piece product in infinite quantity. This is seldom achievable. But anything short of this ideal is inconvenient, involving an array of troublesome tooling, different kinds of machines, temperamental machine operators, quality control problems, material-handling snags, and a host of factory complications.Only if you have been a production supervisor can you appreciate the endless problems and frustrations. If you are unfortunate enough not to have production know-how, recognize your ignorance and be tolerant of production's lack of enthusiasm.

As you talk with production about engineering's tentative plans, the first thing you will learn is production's mild but historic antagonism toward engineering. This is understandable; it is easier for an engineer to draw a part than it is for production to make it. You do yourself and the firm a great service if production is involved in design before it is frozen, so that the individual parts reflect producibility concepts.

After the initial conversation, commence joint design meetings with engineering and production. For the purposes of the proposal, you need agreement on the tentative engineering, the machinery needed and estimated cost, the tooling and estimated cost and lead time, inspection procedures and equipment, etc.

The cost of the finished product is determined largely by these two departments—engineering and production. Purchased materials and components can be priced by the purchasing department. However, the labor cost of machining, assembling, and testing is a function of how it is engineered and how it is made. With the cost target figure in hand, conversations between engineering and production have maximum fruitfulness. The heads of these two departments may be difficult to work with at first, so do not be surprised if a substantial amount of time is spent in working with them. You need a complete master plan for engineering, tooling, and production, including lines of attack, lead time, and costs. However, if the proposal is approved, tentative tooling designs are formed and the tooling is actually built. This may well be the greatest portion of the development cost. So this aspect must be thought through thoroughly— which is usually necessary anyway, in order to arrive at production cost estimates.

GOING ONWARD

Having gotten agreement and planning from engineering and production, then you work with finance, sales, and advertising departments. These three were discussed in the previous chapter. After covering the entire circuit, if all looks good, assemble all the data into a well-illustrated tome with a four-page summary on top, as suggested in the previous chapter. However, the proposal is purely that the company undertake the internal expense of formal *development* of the product. This includes design and engineering, building and testing prototype units, and designing and making the production jigs, fixtures, dies, and other tooling. It does not involve purchase of any significant amount of raw material and it does not involve purchase of any capital equipment. Part of your projected manufacturing cost is the assumption that if capital equipment is needed, those operations involved will be farmed out (using your tooling) or that you will obtain the necessary equipment on short-term leases until your machines arrive. So your proposal is that top management approve development and all operations up to the threshold of production. At that point, everything stops for a final review and approval before going into full-scale production and into sales.

If you have worked thoroughly, covered all the bases, pacified the department heads, kept in touch with your top management, and discussed the project informally with them, then the actual development proposal should find easy sledding. First of all, approval is sought only for a sharply defined total investment. You will not be moving into full-scale production—merely rehearsing for it. You should receive a "yes" or a qualified "yes"—"yes, but wait until the addition is finished." "Yes, but wait until we are out of our busy season" (which you should have known beforehand); etc. If you get a "no," a provisional "no," or just no decision, then you and top management are badly out of phase—and you and a lot of other people have invested much time, energy, and gray matter for no purpose.

PUTTING THE DEVELOPMENT PLAN TO WORK

Having received approval of your proposal to commence development, the first thing is to go into a huddle with finance. The budget for development costs has been approved by the president. Have finance establish separate account numbers for each department which is involved. Against these accounts are charged internal expenses, time, and outside puchases. A copy of the budget for all purchased materials, goods, and supplies goes to purchasing. Between finance and purchasing a close day-by-day control must be set over expenses. Employees of these departments should be instructed to watch the accounts, and if anything exceeds the budget, you should be notified immediately.

Make certain that any questions or complaints which finance or purchasing may have are brought to you—not taken to the department head involved. If that does not sit well, go back to the president and get it in writing. It is extremely important that none of the departments become caught between you and your time schedules on one hand and the finance or purchasing department frowning over invoices on the other. Budget excesses are largely your responsibility—do not forget it.

The proposal to top management included a complete master plan, things to be done. by whom, how long each would take, and how much it would cost. A master time table was included. Copies should be in the hands of all department heads so that each knows what he is to do—and knows what everybody else is doing. Since each department head had an active part in developing the plan, it will be difficult for them now to change their minds or back out. As a matter of principle, schedule meetings with two or three of the department heads for a review every week or two. This may be formal or informal, depending upon the nature of the company and the size of the project. Nonetheless, constant organized reviews are necessary; they must not degenerate into informal catch-as-catch-can meetings with individuals. If a department falls behind schedule, or goes over budget, the head should be forced to explain the reasons to a group consisting of other department heads—not just the new-product manager. Then it is up to you to notify the president.

Since a number of things are going on simultaneously, the new-product manager will be busy. While engineering is refining the final design and making and testing prototype units, the tooling group is finalizing fixturing drawings, production may be making dummy runs to confirm cost estimates, purchasing is ordering components, sales/marketing and the new-product manager are working together on final market research, increasing the accuracy of predicted sales potential, penetration rates, etc. Advertising is working on the copy and art for the literature, direct mail pieces, advertising, and for the technical materials required. Everything necessary before going into full-scale production is being done. This requires a great deal of coordination and constant watching, encouraging, knot cutting, and prodding by the new-product manager.

LAST CHANCE TO RETREAT

After the final stage of the pre-production development work has been finished to everyone's satisfaction, but before you take the baby to the president, have all the department heads meet together—to go over the results of the development project. Compare actual costs with those presented to top management. Compare the final design with that which was expected, and with competitive efforts. The purpose of the meeting is to get everybody involved together, go over the project one last time, make certain that everybody is satisfied and on the right track and that everybody wants to present it to the president.

But if somewhere along the line the whole thing has gone sour, and did not die then, it is best killed at this stage. Naturally, there has been an investment, and for this investment there must be an accounting. However, it is far better to go to the president with an explanation of why the new-product manager and the department heads have mutually agreed to dump the project, than it is to do a cover-up and move knowingly into production when you have a dud.

If everybody is happy, then the new-product manager makes up a supplement to his original tome, refining the data, giving more sophisticated forecasts and more accurate estimates of costs, sales, and profits. The size of the investment is known precisely, as is when this investment must be made. Finance has decided between leasing or purchase of the capital equipment needed.

Everything is ready for management's decision, and all except actual production and sales is either finished or has been tried. Since only selling remains as a forecast, review it once more. For the next 2 or 3 years the new-product department will be extremely involved with actual field selling of the product. Make certain that this is not forgotten—and also make certain that you and the sales department are in agreement as to precisely how you will go about doing this. Furthermore, you should have decided what sales volume represents the cut-off point when the new-product group drops out of the picture and the sales department continues routine sales.

PRESENTING THE PACKAGE TO THE PRESIDENT

This presentation of the new product and the final studies and analyses should also be attended by all department heads. They are not there to review the product—they are there as partners, to support and amplify the new-product manager's presentation. For the presentation, have the revised tome and the four-page summary, the prototype model, competitors' products, charts, graphs, dancing girls—whatever is necessary to put on a worthwhile show. However, the president is not going to approve in a half hour that which has taken most of his department heads six months or so to develop.

He has been watching this project. All kinds of people have eagerly passed on information and tidbits of news. Nothing has gone on without his knowledge or without his approval. Therefore, his approval now is partly symbolic, since if he expected to deliver a "no" he would have stopped the project.

However, the development expense (if properly managed) has been quite modest. The major investment has been for the tooling. And if this cost is extremely high (as it might be for a very complex product or one made from stampings, forgings, injection molded plastic, etc.) much of it may have been held off until after the pre-production approval. Therefore the investment made so far is very modest when compared with the investment which will follow the president's approval. From here on in, the company invests heavily in machinery, inventory, and sales expense. So do not be surprised if the president closes the meeting with a "Gentlemen, I will think about it and let you know." It may be a bit anti-climactic, but it is certainly justified.

After receiving the president's approval to move ahead, with or without modifications to the plan as presented, the action follows the course of the *old* new product, described in detail in Chapter 5. If the new-product manager has done his work honestly and each department has carried its share of the work, with everybody pulling in the same harness, then there is no reason for the product to be anything other than a thundering success.

When the product is delivered to the sales department's door, it enters its most dangerous phase. It is up to the new-product manager to make certain that the first 2 or 3 years of its existence shows strong and constant growth. In the end, the success of the product still rests largely on the new-product manager's shoulders.

Ideas Worth Exploring—No. 5

CYLINDRICAL GRINDING ON A SURFACE GRINDER

Description: A simple but sturdy cast or welded framework containing a live and dead center, for holding work between centers during cylindrical grinding on a surface grinder. The live head could be powered by a built-in waterproof electric motor, or belt or chain-driven from a motor mounted on the end of the grinder table. Provision should be made for accommodating workpieces of different lengths, either by a movable "tailstock" or by using centers of various lengths. A separate table lock would position the table with the center line of the apparatus directly under the spindle, yet the table could be unlocked and moved to one side for loading and unloading.

History: Based on a design developed by the author for a specific purpose a number of years ago.

Marketing Comments: Light-duty devices of this type are now being marketed for tool-room use. However, a heavy-duty, high-speed unit, driven by a motor of adequate horsepower, might find wide application. Almost every machine shop has a surface grinder, but relatively few have cylindrical grinders, although such requirements often arise. For certain small parts, the unit described could be used in production —especially for multidiameter parts.

This is only one of a wide range of accessories employed on and with grinding machines. By and large, manufacturers of grinders ignore the host of accessories which might be sold. Yet an accessory line should increase the value of the average sale. Alternatively, such devices could be sold by any firm selling machine-tool accessories. Grinding-wheel firms also might profitably broaden their interest into machine accessories.

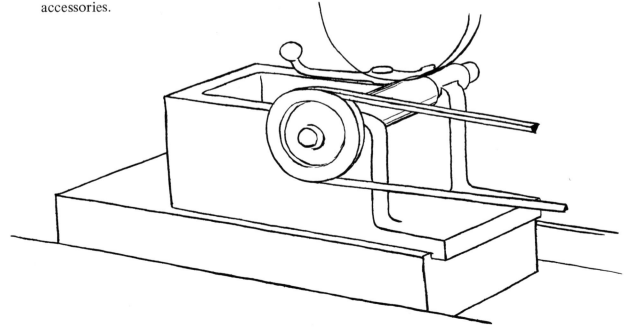

Chapter 7
Sparking the New-Idea Product

> ... although the words "new-product development" usually conjure up visions of test tubes, esoteric research, and technological breakthroughs, the real stuff from which profitable new products are made is usually much more mundane. Ideas, as such, are worthless—only when they can be coalesced into tangible form, when they become *product* ideas, with value, usefulness, and a hoped-for market, are they of interest to the new-product department. Here is how to find ideas—where to look and how to evaluate, how to measure them against marketing opportunity, and how to weigh the real risk against the imagined profits.

WHERE ARE THE FENCES?

Earlier it was suggested that in order to have meaningful new-product development, the president must point the way. In searching for ideas, the new-product department cannot consider the entire spectrum—some narrowing of interests must be made. In previous chapters it was shown how a thinking new-product manager can detect the natural direction of the firm's market/production evolution. This is fine for developing neglected products and copying existing products now made by others. But the likelihood of finding a breakthrough idea in the middle of the company's obvious path is near zero. New-idea products almost always involve long strides into the future in both technology and in marketing. The first question is, "Which way to step?"

New-product development—determining the future course of the company—is one area where the president always holds the reins, even when he delegates them. Others can manage existing products and markets, but only the president can decide the markets which the firm will pursue to assure its continued existence. It is self-evident that the president should impart his preferences to the new-product manager. If the president genuinely has no preferences, then it is up to him to work with the new-product manager and the head of the marketing activity to research, analyze, and then decide which sorts of products and which markets are most appropriate.

The problem, of course, is the nebulous nature of an idea. By definition, an unthought-of-idea cannot be defined. Nor can it even be searched for. All that can be done is to become receptive to ideas—to recognize one when you find it—and then see where it leads. It may lead outside the criteria which the president has established. If so, it is dropped. If it appears to fit inside the fences, it is pursued further. But the fences must exist to make any intelligent sort of idea scanning possible. The logic, thoughtfulness, and care with which the fences are established will have a great deal to do with the success of the firm's new-product activity.

One point should be strongly stressed—the new-idea product differs dramatically from the two classes discussed earlier. In the *old* new product and the *new* new product, the product itself is known, the market is established, data is available, and the guesswork is kept within comfortable limits. An idea has none of these advantages. It may be anything from a new twist on the known to something at the farthest reaches of the unknown. Its usefulness may be readily apparent or it may take considerable exploring to come up with even potential applications.

Most of the excitement about new ideas is myth and exaggeration. You do not go looking for an idea—nor do you wait, spider-like, for one to cross your desk. It just does not happen that way. Or if it does, it happens deep within R&D or in some inventor's subconscious. Even if the new-product manager had or found a genuine breakthrough idea, it would go back to R&D for feasibility research. No, this gossamer stuff is not the raw material for a new product. Fortunately, even when we say new-idea product, a fairly tangible thing is involved. A new-idea product may be something dramatically new, or it can merely be a substantial improvement over existing products. But in any case, it exists—it is not just a disembodied thought, but an idea for a product, with a defined function, assumed usefulness and hoped-for waiting market. Ideas Worth Exploring No. 9 through 14 are typical of useful product ideas: technically-workable ideas, with an apparent market, and (at the moment) no competition.

IDEAS FROM THE FIRM

FROM THE TOP.

One nice thing about the president's new-product ideas; they save a lot of work. If the president has the idea well developed, with sketches or some marketing figures—and particularly if he has already coined a tradename—the question is not whether to go ahead, it is just how fast it can be done. This saves a lot of market research, analysis, meetings, discussions, and approval getting. All the new-product manager has to do is spearhead the project through the shop and then make certain that it is a marketing success.

Of course, the president and other top executives can also pass along legitimate ideas or notes on market opportunities. If they *are* legitimate, they will be very restrained and only mildly suggestive—with no indication of well-constructed preconceptions and no sign of being sponsored. Top executives in any firm have a wide range of contacts with executives of other firms. These people, and others in their usually extensive circle of acquaintances, may pass along very worthwhile ideas. The new-product manager's only problem is in knowing his bosses well enough to know whether this is a "go boy" situation, or a legitimate suggestion from a thoughtful and knowledgeable man. If the latter, of course, the idea follows the same review as any other idea.

RESEARCH DEPARTMENT.

The value of ideas from research depends upon the type of research being done—pure, applied, or none. The mere existence of an R&D department does not mean that research is being conducted. Often "research" is merely an "in" term meaning quality control, application engineering, design engineering, experimental, or even a department without function—merely window dressing for occasional plant tours. If genuine research is being conducted, the department may be a fount of ideas—deliberate solutions to a marketing or technical problem, breakthrough improvements on existing products, and new-product ideas which spin off from other research activity. Often these ideas are patentable. If an idea looks worthwhile, get your patent going, just in case the idea has possible future use. Afterward, if the idea does not fit within the new-product development fences, the patent may be sold outright or licensed to others.

ENGINEERING.

There is a great deal of difference between a scientist and an engineer. From the standpoint of new-product development, the scientist is most interested in ideas, the engineer in things. Engineers are more practical—theirs is an applied science. Department activities stick closely to the mainstream of the firm's product line and engineers tend to think in hardware terms. Without even trying, your engineers output new-product ideas—the job is just to capture them. So get acquainted with as many of the individual engineers as possible. Many times an idea winds up being a doodle on a scratch pad, and is lost forever if the new-product manager's lines of communication are not wide open.

Engineers also get deeply involved in designing and specifying purchased components, factory supplies, machines, and other facilities, so you may find very practical new-product ideas that are considerably afield.

Engineers tend to criticize the work of other engineers. That is, they are much more likely to take a design and try to improve it than they are to assume that it is the ultimate development of the basic idea. For this reason, an idea from engineering is likely to contain excellent sales features.

SALESMEN.

These men, as a class, defy classification. There are engineering types, accountant types, salesmen types; men who sell on ability, on personality, on service, on perseverance, on technical know-how, on entertainment. Some salesmen insist on being experts in the product they sell—others are more comfortable if they know next to nothing. Some are quite content with their company the way it is, and others constantly frustrate themselves by coming up with ideas for new products and new markets which the company could go after.

If the salesmen deal primarily with distributors or with customers only at the purchasing-agent level, new-product ideas are most likely to be of the kinds presented in Chapters 5 and 6—not new ideas as such. However, if the salesmen work with customers' engineers, get out into the customers' plants, or do their own service work, they may come up with completely new ideas. As you get to know the salesmen, seek out the curious and ingenious ones.

The biggest problem with idea-generating salesmen is that the men are often impatient. Unsympathetic with the months of very hard work that goes into analysis and development of a new product, they lose interest before the idea comes to fruition. So if an idea generated by one of the salesmen clears the hurdles and goes into development, be certain to keep him posted.

SHOP PEOPLE.

Men involved in production can be fruitful idea sources—if you can find the right ones. They may be found among the rank-and-file, but they are more likely to be in jobs which require thinking. Practical thinking men usually push their way into the fore and will be found among the union stewards, group leaders, foremen, and supervisors. Also look among setup men, machine repairmen, maintenance men, millwrights, and inspectors.

The new-product manager will be handsomely repaid if he can devote some portion of his time to becoming acquainted with the people who work for his firm, no matter how far away from the mainstream of his working contacts. Because of the broad spectrum of people, interests, and abilities, ideas generated may be of any kind, so do not expect much in usable ideas. But nonetheless, encourage the thinking people to be new-product conscious, since it is these same people who can help when struggling with product redesign, increasing production efficiency, reducing costs, improving quality, etc.

When developing a new product, getting these thinking shop people involved may throw completely new light on design, methods, and production problems. All too often, department heads have risen through the ranks, with very limited experience outside the firm. Thus they know the company's way of doing things, but may be out of touch with the rest of industry. Younger machine operators, who are more mobile as a group, may have broader experience and thereby be able to throw fresh ideas against a problem. So it is a good idea to keep in touch with these people on general principles.

THINKING PEOPLE.

The new-product manager's circle of chance and personal acquaintances are a source of ideas, but since the spectrum of their interest is so broad, there is little likelihood that their ideas will be anywhere near the firm's target area. Nonetheless, when casual acquaintances learn that you are in new-product work it is astonishing the ideas that may be volunteered. In a couple of cases, profitable new product ventures were sparked by conversations with chance seat-partners during airplane flights.

IDEAS FROM IDEAS

PRODUCTS AND CUSTOMERS.

An excellent idea source is hindsight. Sometimes you can get men to open up after they have finished designing, developing, or building something. The question to ask is, "Now that the job is done, have you thought of a better way of doing it?" This may be received with indignant snorts but is just as likely to cause a wry grin and then the volunteering of excellent and worthwhile ideas.

In talking to distributors and customers, a useful conversational gambit (during lunch or some other informal time) is to mention some remote industry or product at random and say, "Now there is a conservative field—I don't think there has been a worthwhile new idea in 20 years." You may get agreement, but you may also get an outpouring of ideas and idea development in a non-related area which will trigger thoughts worth exploring.

IDEA MEN.

This is a favorite possibility. There are men who are bubbling founts of ideas. Some are geniuses or nearly so; others are just plain nuts. As employees they are frustrating. Employed anywhere but in active R&D they are nothing but a nuisance. The problem is that they generate ideas for ideas' sake. Everything they see, everything they work on, half of what they read or hear, generates ideas.

The author has known two such men. The experience was highly frustrating in both cases. Many of their ideas were fascinating (and still are), yet wound up as complete wastes of time—impossible to ignore, but equally impossible to capture and utilize. The new-product manager requires ideas which can be embodied in practicality. Such ideas must either come from minds rooted in practicality or be worked upon by such minds. Pure idea men can seldom provide this practicality. Sometimes the idea itself is practical but of a type that faces astronomical marketing difficulties. Such ideas usually come one-of-a-kind; if pursued they lead the new-product manager on a wild-goose chase.

Worse yet, the idea man is proud of his offspring—and becomes miffed if it is not given proper homage and pursued with some fervor. Such men are dreamers— impractical, ahead of their time, men of the caliber of the Wright brothers, Edison, Goodyear, Ford, Bell, etc. Yes, there may be tremendous ideas among the output of an idea man—but the mountain of chaff which you must wade through to find it discourages the winnowing.

LOOK AROUND.

The new-product manager will establish lines of communication with salesmen, engineers, research, shop people, customers, prospects, and his brother-in-law. But when the dust settles, the most useful ideas will come from himself. Not because he is brilliant, but because he is looking. His screening procedure soon becomes instinctive, automatic, perhaps completely unrealized. Then the ideas that are retained by his mind are the useful ones, those with foreseeable potentials.

The ability to deliberately force-feed the mind, to cause it to put out potentially useful ideas, can be developed. The technique is merely to constantly ask oneself questions. Accept nothing as it stands. Pick any product in a book, or dimestore, trade show, or your wife's kitchen. Ask, "Does this embody any concepts that might be applied to our markets? What if it were ten feet long—or microscopic? Could it be inverted? Why was it made this way? What is...How could...?" Free the mind of conservatism, from restraints, and let it freewheel. Soon the process becomes unconscious—you are only aware of the ideas that "measure up." Like the idea man, the new-product manager becomes a constant source of ideas. The difference is in the direction of their thinking: the idea man starts with an abstract idea and goes off in all directions—the new-product manager starts with ideas from all directions and brings them back to try them in his own field of interest. The difference is significant, because the new-product manager's process yields ideas which can be put to work.

Of course, there is a rub. Ideas are expected to originate in certain sections of the company—R&D, engineering, sales, etc. In the beginning the neophyte new-product manager will probably get better cooperation from these departments if he pretends to find his own ideas among them, sacrificing the "credit" in the interests of the accomplishment. The new-product manager must remember that he is not a manager of products—he is a manager of products while they are *new*. Everything that he starts ultimately must be handled by other people, and their cooperation will be greater if the idea is considered to be their own.

Planting an idea in somebody else's mind (or pretending to find it there) requires a realistically cynical outlook, but it is the most graceful way of getting the long-term job done. Since it is human to claim credit when it is not necessarily due, the "planting" is not difficult. In casual conversation with almost anybody, mention the idea in passing, fully enough to get it across, but not enough to make an issue of it. Do not linger—you want the idea to be recognized, that is all. Let it germinate for a few days and then bring it up again. "You mentioned an idea last week, and the more I think about it . . ." etc. The process is not difficult, unless it contradicts the man's own prejudices and thoughts on the subject. If so, then seek out more fertile soil. Once the idea is well planted, the new-product manager can pick it up and amplify it. Credit goes where it should, well within the ranks of established people, yet the new-product manager has the idea going. Everyone is happy.

BOOKS AND MAGAZINES.

This is the most fruitful of all idea sources. The author's pet searching place is the library—old books and trade magazines. Anything this side of Leonardo da Vinci can be fruitful, although (in metalworking) books published between 1900 and 1930 seem most fruitful. Apparently a great deal of mechanical know-how was lost during the Great Depression when many firms closed. Some were making excellent products which could be marketed today. And pure know-how was lost, too. The experienced engineers and machinists had no apprentices to teach and no way of passing on the "tricks of the trade." By World War II, many of the old timers had retired and those left were working under the forced draft of war production, with no time for leisurely tutoring.

Every year we rediscover (and get patented) products, procedures, and solutions which were known to our grandfathers. Most mechanical technology is not new. If this is doubted, go to any good technical museum and study clocks, precision instruments, firearms, machines, and other mechanical contrivances of 50 to 100 years ago. Study the design, precision, shapes, contours, and surface finish of these old products—then look at the machines available for their manufacture. Do not dismiss this work as "hand fitted." Mass production existed 100 years ago—just as it does today. We can profitably study the accomplishments of this era, because we have forgotten much that was known. Some of this can be regained by analyzing old books. When you start looking at early technical books, the first thing that strikes the eye is the number of products which one assumed to be more recent developments.

Those of you who remember automobiles of the '30s know that many of the features which we consider modern developments were actually a generation old or more when they finally reappeared. In metalworking, things move even more slowly. A scan through a typical old book, *Shop and Foundry Practice,* ICS, 1901, shows an interesting device for centering round stock, a lathe tool-post design which appears superior to the rocker arrangement employed on most tool-room lathes; spade-type reamers; an interesting and probably marketable form of non-deflecting boring bar; a thread-chasing tool (Ideas Worth Exploring—No. 8 in this book); inserted blade cut-off and threading tools; and two types of expanding mandrels now being marketed under current patents! The point is that much has been forgotten. Old books will yield many ideas that might be explored and marketed successfully.

The same, of course, can be said for old magazines. Many trade magazines were published well before the turn of the century. The *Scientific American* was, in its earliest days, almost a house organ for a patent-brokerage firm. Issues published from the end of the Civil War through the turn of the century are full of all kinds of mechanical contrivances—many of which might be the genesis of thoughts for current new products.

Do not dismiss such sources merely because your firm is part of modern technology—plastics, electronics, etc. In 1951, a charge-changing accelerator for use in nuclear research was developed at the University of California at Berkeley—yet the same device was developed and patented in 1937—fourteen years earlier! And even if older books, magazines, and patents do not yield solutions for you, they still may provide market opportunities and ideas. From plastic gadgets to electronic instruments, many modern products are merely today's version of earlier ideas.

In a current vein, look into trade magazines and scientific journals in completely non-related fields. It is not at all unusual for a thinking new-product manager to find an idea in a remote industry which can be developed as a new concept in his own.

PATENTS.

The *Patent Gazette* should definitely be on the new-product manager's subscription list. This 500-odd page weekly book gives one illustration and a very brief description of each patent issued that week. Since the patents are not segregated into specific fields, scanning the *Gazette* exposes you to ideas in every conceivable area. The *Gazette* is over an inch thick and arrives weekly, so the tendency is to flip through it.

This is regrettable, since a careful look at each item exposes the reader to a host of ideas which can spark other ideas.

A patent is granted for only 17 years. Often it takes all or most of that 17 years to get from the invention stage to worthwhile sales volume. Very few patented ideas ever survive the transition. Therefore, if you deliberately analyze *Patent Gazettes* of 17 or more years ago, you can look for ideas that spark better ideas, but you can also look at specific inventions. The ideas in these patents are now fair game.

The patent office can provide lists of government-owned patents and private patents available for licensing. Many people have assured me that this is a direct route to worthwhile product ideas. Under peculiar circumstances, this might be the case.

CAN YOU FIND A PROBLEM?

Ideas are answers, so one approach is to look for problems. "Problem" is "opportunity" spelled backwards. It is part of selling to look for prospects with problems. Unfortunately, it is difficult for the new-product manager to plug into such opportunities since this is part of routine selling. However, talking with salesmen may reveal problems which could not be solved by proper use of the firm's products. If a pattern can be found, it may represent an opportunity. For that matter, a single occurrence may also represent opportunity if the solution has wide usage. But at best, problem seeking is nebulous and frustrating—much easier said than done.

However, surprisingly original ideas can be forced by proposing theoretical problems to good, active minds. Take your present products (or at least, familiar ones) and explore possibilities. This can be almost anything: how to cut manufacturing costs by 50%, grossly improve the operating performance, miniaturize or vastly expand the product or its capacity, make it silent, 100% faster, everlasting, capable of doing impossible jobs, etc. If the "problem" approaches the absurd, thinking is forced out of routine paths and may produce worthwhile new concepts.

To a degree, this technique is used in value analysis. Here a component is taken and its design, characteristics, and production are subjected to free-wheeling discussion to see if gross improvements can be found. Typical results are frequently cited in advertisements, where expensive stampings are evolved into simple parts of formed wire, weldments are redesigned as castings, and castings are redesigned as weldments.

MARKET NEEDS

The old adage in new-product development is, "Find a need—then fill it." That sounds great, but in practice what usually happens is that the new-product manager exposes himself to a vast array of solutions—then goes looking for a suitable problem. If that problem exists in sufficient quantity to make the solution a marketing success, then he has a new product on his hands. If he finds that there are no problems to fit that specific solution, he must create the problem or shelve the idea.

The world "problem" is interesting—just because it is so meaningless. Are problems found—or created?

This is being written with a ball-point pen, which is now in its smear, blob, soon-go-dry stage. That is no problem—it will be replaced with a refill in a little while. Refills are not always consistent—some refills just go dry, without warning. Others smear, leak, and blob their way to an agonizing death. What if one invented a refill guaranteed to give its first blob 500 words before it went dry, with reminder blobs every 50 words until the end? He would have a product with a tremendous sales feature, a real answer to a problem. But is it really a problem (a market need) as such, or does it become one only when some ad agency presents it as one?

If all ball-point pen users stopped buying refills because they blobbed and smeared—or because they didn't, then that would clearly be a market need—a problem. And any firm who could answer it would have a market opportunity. But if all the ball-point pen users are happy except a few oddballs who have this blob/smear hangup, and some refill engineer eliminates it—has he an answer to a problem? Thus, has he found and filled a "need"?

It is this author's opinion that most market "problems" are made, not found—that an operating idiosyncrasy of a product is found and seized upon by men too ignorant to know better. And since they do not know any better, they design away this blemish and voilà!—they have an answer to a problem, a great sales feature, and market opportunity unrolls before them, all green and golden in the sunlight. They go on to make millions, while the engineers of established competitors scowl and mutter in their beer, "Well it wouldn't be a problem if the customer would use the thing properly."

So the ingredients of success in finding and solving market needs appear to be a hypercritical nature, carefully nurtured ignorance, an ability to become enthusiastic over an idea, and a deaf ear to phrases such as, "We've always done it that way"; "It's an operating characteristic"; "The customers don't mind"; "Customers in this business are very conservative and don't like changes." Can this be put to work? Yes.

The new-product manager supplies the critical nature, enthusiasm, deaf ear, and part of the vital ingredient—ignorance. The rest of the ignorance you get from new employees—where else?

New employees are not ignorant, as such—merely ignorant of your firm's ways of doing things and of the history and tradition behind your products. When the firm hires new engineers, service men, or salesmen, try to get acquainted with them. As they begin to fit into the harness, they will see and ask about many things. This attitude gradually drops off, and disappears in about a year or two. By that time, they have fitted into the firm's pattern and they no longer notice those things that seemed so strange at first. But during the first six months, perhaps a year, their comments are interesting and often fruitful sparks for starting ideas.

INTERNAL RESEARCH AND DEVELOPMENT.

This, of course is the classic corporate source for ideas. Unfortunately, research scientists often do not recognize a marketable idea when they have one. Research, unless oriented to some specific problem or for developing some specific thing, often produces a multitude of blind alleys. Each is explored until proven nonproductive, then abandoned. However, what is nonproductive to a research man may be eminently interesting to a new-product man. Further, research people tend to know so much about a given field that they forget the market significance of what they know. The new-product manager goes to R&D with what he thinks is a completely new idea and is greeted with proof that they knew about it 30 years earlier.

Naturally, people in R&D seldom have a well-developed marketing sense; if they were marketing men they would not be in R&D. It is the new-product manager who brings together the marketing feel and the R&D ideas. Since marketable ideas are as likely to be found among abandoned R&D findings as they are along the mainstream of their exploration, the new-product manager must keep track of current projects and get acquainted with the better men.

On a broader scale, the new-product manager should join those technical and engineering societies which are applicable to his fields of interest, attend technical meetings and conferences, and carefully review the technical papers. These often comment on subjects in passing that are well worth exploring. For instance, there has been a great deal of development work performed in the last 20 years on various types of chipbreaker drills. However, in 1917, researchers at the University of Illinois were attempting to determine the optimum helix angle for twist drills. During their study, they tested a number of designs which we would today recognize as chipbreaker types. Since that is not what they were looking for, they did not realize what they found. It was 30 years later before the subject came up again, and it has taken 20 years more to create impact in the market place.

Spade drills have gained acceptance during the last 10 years. Deliberate commercial exploitation assumed effective proportions perhaps in the early '50s. Yet the idea, almost identical to the present-day product, was being made and sold in 1903! But it was not pursued to any extent, was dropped, and then forgotten. It took over 50 years to come full circle again.

How many good ideas have been lost, unrecognized, or misfiled at your firm during the last 2 or 3 decades? Ideas that are old hat to experienced engineers and research men might be considered breakthroughs by customers.

READ-READ-READ.

The new-product group should resign itself to being the originators of 75% or more of the worthwhile new-product ideas, in spite of everything they do to encourage generation of ideas from other people. The fact that most of their ideas must be planted in other minds, in order to get them into the proper end of the accepted channels, is beside the point. Since the new-product group must generate ideas, they must expose themselves to enough information to make this possible. Usually the answer is reading. Conversations can be fertile, but since one's circle of contacts is always limited, this soon runs dry, then becomes incestuous.

Concentrate on books, magazines, technical papers—new, old, and extremely old. There are excellent precedences for looking at old ideas. The Gatling gun was invented in 1861, then was dropped when Maxim invented the true machine gun, which was much faster. Yet, 100 years later, when the Maxim machine gun had reached its ultimate development, the Gatling gun concept of independent rotating barrels was resurrected for aerial guns to give the barrels time for cooling between rounds. This was hailed as a brilliant innovation—and it was. But even more brilliant was the idea of using an old idea to solve a new problem. Books and magazines, of any date, are full of ideas.

But when you search for something, look for it where it exists. A few years ago there was a great deal of excitement about the abominable snowman. Sir Edmund Hillary went to the frozen peaks of the Himalayas to see if he could find it. Its tracks had been reported there, so that is where he looked. But when he found nothing in the icy expanses, he concluded that it did not exist. Whether it exists or not, common logic should have told anyone that no large animal lives in the frozen ice. It may go there, crossing the ice to get somewhere else, but if you want to find it you should at least start by searching where there is food, water, and shelter.

So it is with ideas. If you want new ideas do not look in the current trade magazines—they just tell you what somebody else has developed. Look in the places where unrecognized ideas lurk—old books, books in completely unrelated fields, scientific journals, trade journals from other industries, technical papers about remote subjects. If you want completely new, innovating breakthrough ideas look for them where you will find them—far afield.

IS IT REALLY IDIOTIC?

Some ideas smell good, others do not. Unfortunately, no two people react the same way to an idea. When an idea is first mentioned, it is often dismissed or scoffed at. This is unfortunate, but must be expected; the new-product manager must have a thick skin.

But, of course, the idea must have intrinsic soundness—or at least be a basis upon which soundness can be constructed. It is not easy to determine the value of a new-product idea, or even its practicality. Most of the products which we use unthinkingly were idiotic ideas at one time. If you have a far-out idea, do not let it be killed by scoffers. There are two directions to proceed in reducing it to practice: 1. Do it yourself. 2. Get help. The first route is suicidal, so actually there is no choice.

Know your people. Then, when you come up with a wild-eyed idea, take it to this man in R&D, engineering, or sales. You need support, another affirmative opinion, one whose position in the firm is well established and whose assistance "counts." Obviously, he must have an open, receptive mind, some marketing sense, and both vision and optimism. If the idea appeals to him, you are at the first of the many steps which may lead ultimately to development.

EVALUATING IDEAS

DOES IT FIT INSIDE THE FENCES?

Finding an idea is the easy part. Deciding what to do with it is considerably more difficult. Some ideas seem to go nowhere, leading toward completely wrong markets— or they may simply appear to be nonmarketable. Other ideas are so broadly applicable that it is difficult to decide whether they are worthwhile marketing. For instance, in this book is described an interesting form of rotary electrical connection, utilizing roller bearings (Ideas Worth Exploring No. 9). This idea might be marketable and it might not be. A firm might incorporate the idea into a larger product and find it well worthwhile—but that makes it a detail, not a new product. In short, the value of this idea depends upon the firm—whether they are manufacturing components, a broad range of electrical fittings, or machine tools.

Most ideas fall naturally into or outside the target area. The difficult ones are those which hit the area, yet also have broader appeal. For instance, visualize a firm selling metalworking drill presses through stocking industrial distributors. The firm develops and patents a smaller, high-speed drill press. It fits their market, distribution, and their sales force. No problem. However, upon analysis, three new markets are discovered, each untapped by the company. The machine has applications in the aerospace industry, not served by the present distributors. Second, it could be used in automotive service and repair—garages—another market not covered by the distribution. Third, it is fine for woodworking, although the firm is not set up to pursue this market. Further, when the patent was granted a couple of firms, not direct competitors, extended feelers about buying on a private-name basis or becoming patent licensees.

What does the new-product manager do with this potpourri? Should he ignore these broader market potentials? Should he suggest a second layer of sales and distribution to take advantage of them? Ideas which straddle the fence pose knotty problems. The problems are always solvable—but the solution is always a compromise that seldom satisfies everybody.

SHOULD THE FENCE BE CUT?

If you have a product that looks good, yet goes beyond the target areas as defined by top management, think carefully before proceeding. Your best bet is to hold the broader market concepts in abeyance until the decision to develop the product is behind. If the answer is "yes," and the product moves into development, then go to top management and discuss your estimate of these broader market opportunities.

Extensive market research and analysis will probably be needed to establish and measure these markets—the farther away from home base, the more expensive this will be. Therefore, top management's approval should be obtained before starting. They may decide that they are just not interested. Be certain that the question is kept distinct from the decision to proceed on development. The question is merely is it worthwhile looking outward at a broader market—or is it not? The president's answer settles the question.

In spite of this good advice, there are cases where the new-product manager might do some low-powered analysis, even on markets that are far afield. This occurs when an idea looks good, but is obviously outside the target area. The possibility exists that the *idea* might be patented, developed, and then sold or licensed to some other firm. In this case, the new-product manager might decide to make preliminary studies so that he has something to talk about when he approaches his top management.

PRELIMINARY EVALUATION.

When a dramatically new idea for a product has been found, one which would fit within the market fences, the next step is preliminary evaluation—getting a feel for the product and its potential sales and profits. The more genuinely new the idea is, the more difficult this preliminary evaluation will be.

As shown before, a full-scale proposal to management is a serious undertaking. Before proceeding, the new-product manager must take a very careful look at the idea in hand—and how it may fit his firm and its people.

If the new-product manager decides to drop the idea, he may be passing up a potentially profitable addition to the firm's business. On the other hand, it will take time (which is money) to dig more deeply. This is a crucial decision for a man to make alone. If the manager has a smoothly functioning, skilled, and experienced staff, the matter can often be discussed and settled within the group. However, if the new-product manager runs alone, the idea should be discussed with other people in the firm, in order to invite opinions which may either cancel or reinforce his own.

In a sense, this is merely spreading the responsiblity. But others may see new facets. point out unnoticed strengths/weaknesses, or otherwise throw new light upon the idea. Besides, a corporation consists of many people—the new-product manager must get their initial reaction to the idea. The decision is his alone, but the opinions of others help in making it.

CAN IT BE SOLD?

Market data for a nonexistent product is also nonexistent. If the new idea replaces some present type of product, it may be possible to get significant data by doing market analysis and making a volume forecast for the present product. If there is no appropriate product to measure, then the job is to estimate the number of uses or applications for the new idea. Between these two approaches, useful results should be obtainable. Often both should be explored briefly to be certain which method is more applicable. Finding the proper thing to measure, and then deciding how to use the measurement, will take some thinking. As with other considerations, the farther the new product departs from established products and methods, the more difficult (and vital) this thinking becomes.

For instance, visualize the problem facing the firm which introduced the first nailing machine. Statistics on usage of nails—or sales of hammers—would have been meaningless. The question was, "How many firms and contractors do large volume nailing under conditions where a power nailer could be used—and where it would pay off?" For such a question, the only answer obtainable is a guess—and the more people guessing, the better. Out of the guesses comes some estimate of the total number of *potential* customers—the theoretical 100% saturation number. The next task is to estimate the penetration (%) for each of the first five years.

A completely new idea requires hard selling for an extremely long period of time. Unlike the classes of new products in Chapters 5 and 6, the education and introductory phase for a dramatically new industrial product may stretch into decades.

For instance, carbide tools are well known and widely accepted in metalworking today. However, if you take a careful look into a few plants, you will find many good but unrealized applications for carbide tools. Perhaps in some of these cases, carbide was tried and for one reason or another difficulty was encountered. But in the majority of them, carbide has never been tried. The carbide firms and other makers of carbide cutting tools have chalked up fantastic sales gains, yet their market spreads ever broader before them. This has been a long hard pull, requiring tremendous advertising and sales pressure over many years. Carbide tools have been aggressively sold, accepted, and acclaimed by customers for over 30 years—yet the end of the educational job is still out of sight, far into the future.

The necessity for educational promotion, the extremely adverse sales-cost/profit ratio on a product that requires constant education, and the problems in interesting and then training the sales force/service men/distributors/customers—all these are disadvantages of a dramatically new product. The internal starting-up expenses and the staggering cost of sales may mean that the product will not break even for a long time—it is not unusual to find the breakeven period extending out 5, 10 or more years. By and large, American industry is extremely conservative and very, very slow to accept radically new ideas. So the new-product manager must approach the decision to pursue a completely new concept with both eyes open.

One of the shortest routes to failure is to develop, introduce, and try to market a product which is ahead of its time. Of course, one cannot say that a company should not be an innovator—all progress would stop if brave men did not struggle with spreading the gospel for new concepts. Nonetheless, the new-product manager, working to increase his company's profits, must realize that profits from a dramatically new product are extremely illusive, far in the future, and almost impossible to predict. Most genuine breakthroughs that come to mind—Polaroid, Xerox, etc., were inventions of individuals and the company involved grew up around the marketing of the new concept. That is a world away from having a firm, now busy doing something else, spearhead a major new concept—and make a profit doing it.

SCRATCH-PAD ENGINEERING.

Assuming the basic idea is feasible—that it does not need laboratory verification of its practicality— the next step is to begin reducing it to hardware. Ask engineering to do highly informal scratch-pad sketching, establishing the broad parameters, and exploring the different ways in which the concept might become a product. All that is needed is to pull together rough notes on the general appearance, capacity, function, and specifications of the product. Not enough to inhibit free, uncommitted thought at a later date—just enough to flesh out the idea, make it real, and verify its compatibility with present manufacturing equipment. Since costs are all-important, the new-product manager should get tentative cost estimates or comparisons with present products.

If the product is complex, it may be that alternate designs or mechanisms will be found, and that prototype components must be made and tested. If so, the new-product manager must interest engineering and R&D in cooperating while these tests are conducted. Since R&D are more likely to have the interest (and presumably the facilities), for testing alternate design approaches, it may be best to have engineering sketch out potential designs and then take them back to the laboratory for the tests. If the lines of communication between engineering and R&D are open, this is the best assurance of a good product and early firming of the design.

As the design begins to take form, invite production to look it over. They may be able to point out potentially troublesome operations or features. More particularly, you need estimates of the type of tooling needed, a guess at its cost, and the manufacturing cost of the product.

Both R&D and engineering know the highly tentative (almost speculative) status of the idea. Production engineering, not having been involved in the idea's pre-natal stages, may not appreciate this, and must be made to do so. It is extremely important that the new-product manager keep his cards on the table. The "product" is merely a jelled idea—nothing more.

THE DOLLAR SIGNS.

From here on the preliminary work is downhill. The labor cost, cost of components and of production facilities are reasonably well established. The new-product manager has some quantity "guesstimates" and the costs have been estimated at these various production levels. From this he looks toward a logical selling price.

However, the pricing of a dramatically new product should not use the established ratios between cost and sales price. One reason is that the cost of sales and service will be astronomical when compared to established products. If the sales manager and new-product manager assume a total sales and advertising expense 3, 5, or even 10 times as great as that of established products, they may still fall short of actuality. Yet management will want the initial investment recovered as quickly as possible, and all concerned want the product to make money. So a fast-building sales volume is vital. The new product, being new and advanced, will attract customers who make their profits from staying ahead of the pack—and it will be repellent to customers who profit by being part of the pack. All these facets, shifting and difficult to assess, will affect the best price for obtaining the optimum sales-volume/profit mix.

In pricing a completely new-idea product, there are a number of different philosophies found. One of them is to establish the selling price as low as possible to discourage competition. Generally, however, this is not wise; it means a very long breakeven period. If the idea is well protected by patents, competition is of minor importance—and pricing is not the best way to discourage them anyway. Frankly, if the concept is a complete breakthrough, and a great deal of long-term customer education is necessary, the better course is to invite competition. Customers are much more likely to become interested in a new concept which appears to sweep the industry than they are if only one voice is raised in the wilderness. If your firm commands the industry, you can do without help. But if you are not number one, then license or private-brand the product—but get help. You can worry about competition some time in the distant future when the market is filled up with excess volume and competition becomes keen—if this ever happens.

In the meantime, the best course is to set a sales price which is realistic in view of the extremely high sales cost, one which accelerates the breakeven period as much as possible, yet does not make the product a poor investment. In short, a price which is "what the traffic will bear" and still be a good (irresistible, if possible) investment for the customer.

The all-important number, of course, is sales volume. How many units can be sold the first year, the second year, and how fast will the entire thing grow? No one knows the answer to this. The best that a new-product manager can hope for is to obtain a guess from sales, play it against his own, and hope that between them they bear some faint resemblance to what will actually transpire.

The best course is to list names of as many potential customers as possible, with the volume of their potential purchases, then assume that perhaps 2, 5, or 10% of these firms might be persuaded to try the new product during the first year. This gives some realistic feeling as to sales volume, and the list of known prospects can be extrapolated against the list of unknown prospects.

Another point which should be discussed (where applicable) is whether to make up the new product in trial quantities and invite customers to use them at little or no cost, or whether to go for broke and assume that when the product is available in quantity, the customers can be found for it. This is an important decision. Field trials will be necessary in any case. But whether these are prototypes and the testing done as part of the engineering development, or are first production runs and the "test" is merely a conditional sale, is an important distinction. Guarantees and warranties may be part of the picture, and should be anticipated.

The sales problem is a complex one—therefore, the advertising problem will be also. Advertising has been presented earlier, in Chapter 5, and will be supplemented in Chapter 14. But promotion of a completely new concept poses one significant difference from that of familiar products—education. Three promotional tools are very effective for introducing new concepts, although they are often left out of campaigns for existing products. These are trade shows, magazine publicity, and talks. Trade shows let prospects walk in, look at the new product, handle it, convince themselves that it exists, and see proof of its value to them. They can indicate their interest, ask questions, talk about potential applications, get quotes, and place orders.

Publicity, in the form of a campaign of full-length magazine articles, is used extensively by smart marketers when pushing new concepts. For instance, if you are an active reader of metalworking magazines, think back over the last ten years. You will recall a constant stream of articles on throw-away carbide tooling, N/C machinery, gun drilling, EDM, titanium, powder metallurgy, inert-gas welding, in-plant slitting lines, "abrasive machining," abrasive belt grinding, and wire brushing. The last two campaigns burned out a few years back, but were heavy at one time. This constant article coverage, plus heavy advertising and selling, is what it takes to sell a concept. The trade magazines are the greatest asset that a totally new product can have. It is impossible to estimate how long it would take even a major firm to familiarize industry with a completely new concept if they did it by direct selling alone.

The third leg on the stool is to take full advantage of the many opportunities to talk to an audience about the new concept. This means getting capable speakers to deliver technical papers at society meetings and to give somewhat less formal talks at meetings of local chapters of the various engineering societies, purchasing agents, and other groups which would contain prospects. Cost is nil (except for travel), inconvenience is high, value is extremely high. This is a valuable but too-often neglected promotion opportunity.

DIG IN OR FORGET IT?

All this has merely been a lead up to the decision—one which only the new-product manager can make. And that is whether or not he should do a serious, in-depth, formal investigation of the new-product idea with the intention of presenting management with a proposal and plan for developing and marketing the product. The new-product manager will make this decision alone. But he would be foolish not to take the accumulated weight of his preliminary exploration and discuss it with key department heads.

The preliminary conversations have not taken any significant amount of time—and next to no money has been invested other than some minor research expenses, which presumably their budget is structured to cover. However, a formal investigation does involve money. It involves a great deal of time by both the new-product manager and the department heads. It means tentative engineering, accurate cost estimates, full-scale investigation of production operations, selection of machines and equipment, roughing out details of tooling design so that costs can be estimated, deciding precisely how the product is to be made, assembled, inspected, packaged, shipped, etc. It means a thorough market research, sales forecasts, investment analysis, and financial forecasts. It involves building prototype units for field trials.

If at all possible these field trials should be conducted even before presenting the new product to top management. The more advanced the concept, the more vital the field tests become. Of course, you will test the product internally—but such tests are nursemaided. It is axiomatic that if anything can go wrong with a new product, the customer will make it happen. Perhaps the product is so complicated or temperamental that the customer, in his inexperience, is incapable of using it properly. If so, you have a major design/marketing/education problem on your hands. Further, if the customer finds it difficult to use the new product profitably, the sales force is bound to shy away because they can foresee all kinds of misunderstandings, problems, complaints, rejections, service calls, etc. So the field trails are inescapable.

If the decision is made to do a formal investigation, the cost of the field trials—in products submitted, travel time, salesman time, etc.—may become formidable. Even the development of tentative operator manuals, instruction sheets, application guides, and service manuals may amount to a substantial sum. The formal investigation costs money—much work must be done just to verify the truthfulness of the proposal to management.

The new-product manager is now at the moment of decision. He must decide "yes," he will go ahead with a formal investigation or "no," he should dump the idea and forget it. If he has excellent rapport with his top management, and has access to them for informal chats, he may well be tempted to discuss it with them. Not to get a decision, but to get their reactions as to whether or not he should continue his investigation. This is risky for two reasons. One, the new-product manager should be in a position to make this decision for himself. Two, top management would have nothing to go on other than the flimsy straws of the preliminary investigation and are almost forced to have a negative reaction. They are inundated with half-baked schemes and poorly considered suggestions. Do not add yourself to the ranks of those who waste the president's time. The new-product manager must make this decision himself. That is part of his job and if he abdicates it he does less than justice to his position.

If the new-product manager decides to plunge ahead, then the new concept is pursued through all the stages of formal investigation. Ultimately this culminates in a presentation of a formal proposal to management, inviting a decision on whether or not to proceed with complete development.

Thus, the new-idea product moves from here to the point where Chapter 6 began: the formal investigation. Once all the steps in Chapter 6 have been pursued to their ultimate conclusion, the product then shifts to the beginning of Chapter 5. These three Chapters—5, 6, and 7—have been assembled in order of increasing complexity and increasing distance from the market place when the new-product idea is begun. When used together (but in reverse order) they cover the entire route for a *profitable,* completely new product.

Ideas Worth Exploring--No. 6

HEAVY-DUTY GRINDING WHEEL

Grinding usually involves extremely light stock removal and a number of passes to finish the workpiece. Modern practice does not make this mandatory, but most users are perhaps overly cost-conscious, and avoid heavy feeds because the wheels break down rapidly. Yet there are many applications where heavy stock-removal could be most attractive for the user. A grinding wheel of the sort shown would be tremendously useful—and probably quite marketable.

One side of the wheel would be developed for the optimum combination of extremely heavy stock removal and minimum wheel wear. The balance of the wheel would be the finishing section, mated to the rougher for approximately even wheel wear, but with much finer grain size for imparting the finish desired. The rougher side takes the heavy cut and the other side semifinishes. On the return pass, the finer side produces the final finish while the roughing side clears the work. Probably a few high grains on the roughing side would leave marks, so the wheel is visualized as primarily for extremely heavy stock removal, rather than for fine surface finish. In use, the wheel might be relieved in the center by dressing, to equalize wear, for better coolant application, and to relieve pressure.

History: A doodle of the author some years ago when tooling a job requiring heavy one-pass stock removal. However, since then a "sandwich" wheel has been seen, which appears to embody this principal. It appears technically feasible—and an idea well worth exploring.

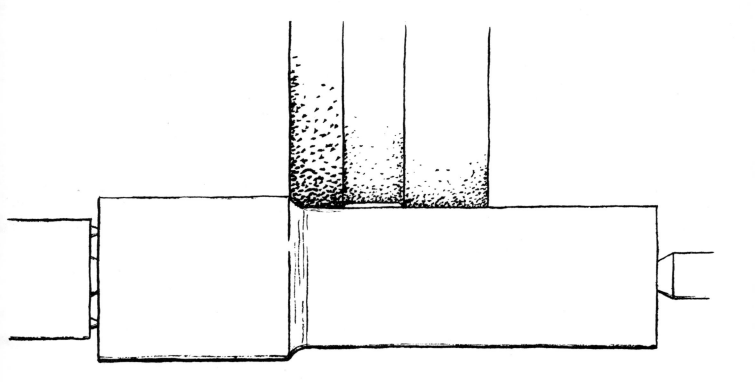

NOTE: This is one of a number of "Ideas Worth Exploring" presented in this book. The author *has not* done this exploring. If a patent is known, it is listed. No listing does *not* mean that the idea is unpatented, or that it can be legally used in any way. Most good ideas have been patented, at one time or another. Most patents have expired and many current ones could probably be contested if literature research turned up prior exposure, as would certainly be the case with many ideas, particularly in the older fields, such as mechanical. *Nevertheless,* none of the ideas given in this book are represented as being free of patents—and the author accepts no responsibility or liability from the use of any of these ideas.

SECTION III
Details About Detail Areas

Chapter 8
Doing It by the Book

> ... by its ill-defined nature, any new-product project deteri-
> orates quickly into complete chaos unless it is held firmly to
> a preconceived master plan and schedule. Here is how to
> draft a plan that the firm can live with, and how to derive a
> schedule and target dates from it.

THE CLASSIC MASTER PLAN

In new-product development, as in other projects, planning and scheduling are interwoven. The plan must contain deadlines for two reasons. First, without tight deadlines, the work would expand to fill the maximum time available—which means that next to nothing happens between the president's crack-the-whip meetings. Second, time is money—the cost of the project is a function of the time devoted to it. The reason why many projects run away from their budgets and take so long to complete is in faulty scheduling/planning. Poor planning is a particular weakness of most companies—which is to say a weakness of most men.

The problem is simply that a project is not thought through in detail—men plunge into the work, substituting their sense of equilibrium and a faith in happy endings for deciding in advance what work needs to be done. Occasionally a project plan is actually committed to paper, but it is usually of the sketchiest sort, listing only the major steps, without any of the messy details. And since the details are left out, they are forgotten or run over blithely; thus everyone underestimates both the complexity of the project and how long it will take. A month after the "action plan" goes into effect it is already running late. Another month later, confusion sets in. Finally the project either sinks to the bottom, to be carried along at the normal glacial speed of the firm's movement, or one strong man takes the project under his wing (to everyone's loud dismay but actual

141

relief) and completes it as he sees fit. In this way, planning becomes a major contributing factor to the failure of most new-product ventures.

It would be usual at this point to give another of those "typical" master plans for a new product. But a genuine working plan is many pages long and is uniquely tailored for one specific product at one point in the moving history of one individual firm—it therefore has no value to anyone else. However, the nature of a real plan, the type of thinking necessary in order to create a plan, can be demonstrated:

THE CLASSIC MASTER PLAN

MASTER PLAN—Change Light Bulb in Bathroom

Project initiated by: Wife
Primary responsibility: Husband
Review and approval: Wife
Deadline desired: Now
Expected completion date: Tomorrow

1. Analyze work involved.
   A. Determine type of fixture.
   B. Height from floor—is ladder needed?
   C. Type of bulb: incandescent or fluorescent?
2. Purchase components.
   A. Bulb in pantry?
   B. If not, insert Subplan No. 1 (obtaining supplies).
3. Assemble tools.
   A. Cigarettes and matches.
      1. Get from kitchen drawer.
      2. If out, insert Subplan No. 1 (obtaining supplies).
   B. Screwdriver (alternate to 3C).
      1. Determine size and type (regular or Phillips).
      2. Get from basement (may combine with other operations).
   C. Pliers (alternate to 3B).
      1. Get from basement (see 3B2).
   D. Bulb (get from pantry).
      1. If necessary, see 2B.
   E. Step ladder (alternate to 3F). If necessary, see 1B.
      1. Get from garage.
         a. Get garage keys first.
   F. Chair (alternate to 3E). If necessary, see 1B.
      1. Get from dining room.
4. Carry bulb and tools to worksite, lay on floor. (Alternate: Lay on vanity counter, or top of toilet tank if more convenient. Decision to be made at time, does not affect rest of plan except Step 11A).
5. Light cigarette and think about job.
6. Place step ladder or chair under fixture. If necessary, see 1B.
7. Mount ladder or chair/step up to fixture (selection depends upon 1B).

8. Examine fixture, confirm type and location of globe fasteners, hand test for tightness.
   A. If loose, grasp globe in left hand, remove fasteners (alternate to Steps 8B, 9, and 10). Go to Step 11.
   B. If loose, grasp globe in left hand, remove part of fasteners; shift hands, remove balance of fasteners. (Alternate to 8A, 9, and 10). Go to Step 11.
   C. If not loose, and proper tools at hand, go to Step 9.
9. Dismount ladder, step back from fixture (alternate to 8A and 8B).
   A. Secure proper tool (screwdriver or pliers).
   B. Return to position in Step 7.
10. Fasteners not loose, remove with tool (alternate to 8A and 8B).
   A. Same as 8A except using tool (alternate to 10B).
   B. Same as 8B except using tool (alternate to 10A).
11. With globe, fasteners and tools in hands, dismount ladder/chair and step back.
   A. Lay globe in safe place (floor, hand basin, vanity counter, top of toilet tank). Decision to be made at time, does not effect rest of plan except Step 4.
   B. Carefully place fasteners in/alongside of globe.
      NOTE:
      1. If globe is in hand bowl, *do not* drop fasteners alongside.
      2. If globe is on toilet tank, *do not* drop fasteners in bowl.
   C. If fasteners are lost through poor supervision/workmanship/failure to observe notes to step 11B, insert Subplan No. 2 (search through boxes in garage to find replacement screws. Possible alternates are retriever tool, use of fingers, screwdriver, magnet, gum on string, etc.).
12. Take 5-minute break (alternate to Step 13).
13. Get can of beer.
   A. If out, insert Subplan No. 1 (obtaining supplies).
Etcetera

Any man with a wife and a bathroom can complete this plan. It is a detailed, working plan for a simple operation. The development of a new product is an extremely complex operation—but the planning principle is the same. Of course, the development plan must allow for simultaneous activity in two or more departments—just envision three union men working together to replace the light bulb in the sample plan given above. Notice that the plan is open—it is known before the job begins that there are alternates to some steps and for other steps certain contingencies are foreseen and allowed for.

The drafting of a complete plan requires nothing except familiarity with the work to be done, intelligence, and time to think the project through. Throughout this book, the vital importance of cooperation with and between department heads has been stressed. Planning puts this cooperative effort to work.

The plan for each department is roughed out with the department head, then the department plans are integrated into a total master plan. When this is finished, go over it, from beginning to end, with each department head, smoothing out the rough spots and correcting for anything missed. The master plan must be approved by all concerned. If the plan is to work, it must *NOT BE imposed upon the department heads by the new-product manager.*

It is quite remarkable how smoothly everything goes when a fully detailed master plan is drawn up, approved, and put into effect. Firms that cannot put on a decent employee picnic are suddenly capable of faultless development projects—just because everyone knows what he is doing, when to do it, and what to do next.

SCHEDULING ALWAYS WORKS IN BOOKS

This is probably a good thing, because it seldom does in practice. Why?—optimism, pride, forgetfulness, and poor planning. Optimism, in that most people are polite. They want to please, to tell the hearer (reader) what he wants to hear. Pride, in that if we estimate eight weeks and the hearers look disappointed, we cut it to six. Forgetfulness, in that complications are overlooked and contingencies are not anticipated. And poor planning, in that it is impossible to make up an intelligent schedule without a plan. However, even with a careful plan, do not expect too much from a time schedule. It will not tell when the project will be completed.

The plan incorporates numerous alternates and allows for many contingencies, but there is no way of knowing in advance which alternate may be followed or which contingency may arise. Therefore, a schedule cannot possibly predict the finish date. What it does is give a minimum and maximum time for each phase of the project, and thus, for the total.

With a carefully thought out and agreed-upon plan, a realistic schedule is not at all difficult. Here is the schedule for our sample plan:

SCHEDULE: Change Light Bulb in Bathroom

| | | | | Time in Minutes | |
Step	Operation		(Odds)	Alternates	Contingencies
1	Analyze	2-5			
2	Components	3-5			
B	Bulb		(1:10)		45
3	Tools A	1-1			
3A2			(1:20)		10*
B or C		5-10			
D		3-5			
E			(1:10)		5-15
F			(1:2)		1-3
4	Carry - time included with Step 3				
5	Cigarette	3-20			
6, 7	Ladder				0-1 1/2
8	Fasteners A		(1:2)	1/2-2	
	B		(1:4)	1-3	
9, 10	Same, with tools				
	A		(1:8)	2-3**	
	B		(1:6)	2-5**	
11	Place globe 1-2				
C					5-120
12	5-minute break	3-10			
13	Beer	1-3			
A			(1:20)		10*

Total Minimum Time 22 1/2

Greatest Maximum Time   66 1/2 (slowest alternate, no contingencies)

Absolute Maximum Time   4 hr. 31 (slowest alternate, all contingencies)

Estimated Actual Time   45 minutes

* If done with contingency for Step 2B, 3A2, or 13A. If done alone, add 35 minutes.

** Alternate to Step 8, but allow 1/2 minute for testing and decision making if Step 8 fails.

Each element has a reasonable time span (min/max) assigned to it, as determined in meetings with the department heads. A similar time span is estimated for contingencies and alternates. Then determine where in the pursuit of each alternate it may be found unworkable and shifting to another made necessary. Then estimate the odds for each alternate being employed and the likelihood of each contingency occurring.

Naturally, these odds estimates will be vague, but when a number of individual estimates for time and likelihood are assembled into an overall total it produces a schedule of remarkable accuracy. The project will probably be broken into a number of phases—end of R&D, of design engineering, of tooling, etc. For each phase, add the minimum and maximum time, then add each alternate and contingency. When played against the likelihood of each one occurring, schedule dates can be assigned. The dates should give the *minimum* estimated time, the *maximum* time, and the *estimated* time. The last is derived by playing the odds figures against the time for the various alternates and contingencies.

In the sample, the minimum time is 22½ minutes, the greatest maximum 66½, and the average is 44½ minutes. Alternates have odds of 1:2 to 1:6 and account for up to 5 minutes. Contingencies range from 1:2 odds on 3F (adds 1 to 3 minutes) to 1:20 odds at 3A2 and 13A (either will add 45 minutes). In sum, the best possible time would be 22½ minutes, the worst conceivable 4 hours 31 minutes, and the estimate about 45 minutes.

Assembled in this fashion, the schedule is easy to monitor and there are no valid reasons why any phase should run later than anticipated. A great benefit is the reasonableness of the schedule—it is a prediction, not a goal. The department heads are not suddenly put under great pressure if they find one route unfeasible and have to shift or start over. This has been anticipated and the schedule permits additional time if it should become necessary. As the work progresses, the estimates are replaced with the actual time and the schedule becomes self-correcting as the applicability of the alternates and contingencies passes and they are eliminated.

Of course, a complicated long-term project involves an equally complex planning and scheduling procedure. Fortunately, there are tools available—PERT and CPM. These are sketched briefly in Figure 8-1. The only point to be made here is that these are tools—not crutches. A firm that cannot plan without PERT will not be able to plan with it. But planning is not difficult—it is merely thought-demanding and time-consuming.

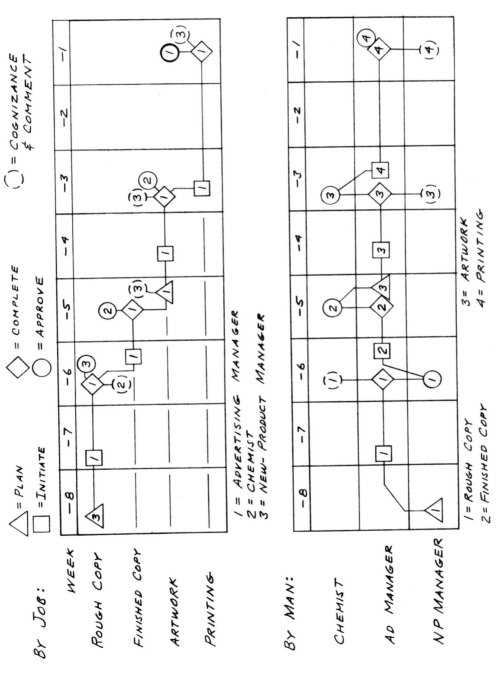
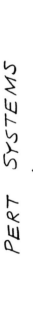

Figure 8-1A

PERT—Program Evaluation Review Technique—is a valuable planning and scheduling tool. The version shown here is highly simplified for illustration—and is modified by using different symbols, either for various activities or various responsibilities. The standard PERT form is like that shown in demonstrating CPM, with each activity referenced to a master chart. As can be seen, the modified versions are easier to understand and are much more intelligible to unsophisticated users.

The best course is to employ conventional PERT for the master plan, then develop modified PERT charts for each man or each activity. In this way you get the best of both concepts.

146

CPM = CRITICAL PATH METHOD

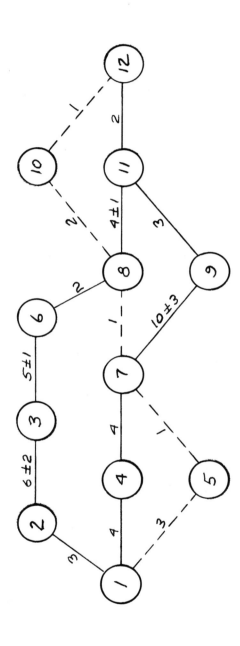

UPPER PATH $3+6+5+2+4+2 = 22 | \pm 2 \pm 1 \pm 1 = \pm 4 | 22 \mp 4 = 18 \longrightarrow 26$

LOWER PATH $4+4+10+3+2 = 23 | \pm 3 | 23 \pm 3 = 20 \longrightarrow 26$

BEST TIME   18 WEEKS
WORST TIME   26 WEEKS

Figure 8-1B

147

CPM is merely a way of determining the time required for the total job. The time for each operation is established and the lowest sum is the minimum possible total time.

Ideas Worth Exploring--No. 7

EXPANDING MANDREL

Description: A mandrel consisting of a slotted steel arbor; the slots milled and ground at a depth which tapers from one end to the other. In each slot rides a hardened and ground jaw, with the jaws held in relative alignment by a cage.

Application: The lathe workpiece is slipped over the mandrel jaws and then the work and jaws are moved along the arbor until the jaws are forced outward to clamp the work. For stability, the jaws should have a certain maximum projection. However, one expanding mandrel of this type could have a fairly wide diameter range. The mandrel has obvious other uses: holding a cutting tool such as a milling cutter or saw, plus uses farther afield—holding tubes, spools, winding cores; or as the basis for a clutch or brake, tube or pipe plug, etc.

History: A book entitled *Shop and Foundry Practice,* Vol. 1; a textbook by the International Correspondence School of Scranton, Pa. The issue in the author's library is the second edition, dated 1901. See also Patent #2,544,633.

Marketing Comments: This should be an excellent product for firms making lathes or lathe tools. It could be sold as a standard item, with the mandrel and replacement jaws stocked by distributors. With minor engineering, the basic concept might be applied to special mandrels, designed for specific applications.

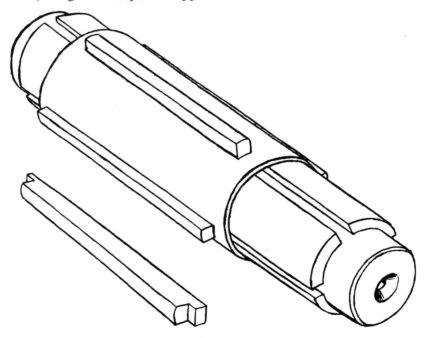

NOTE: This is one of a number of "Ideas Worth Exploring" presented in this book. The author *has not* done this exploring. If a patent is known, it is listed. No listing does *not* mean that the idea is unpatented, or that is can be legally used in any way. Most good ideas have been patented, at one time or another. Most patents have expired and many current ones could probably be contested if literature research turned up prior exposure, as would certainly be the case with many ideas, particularly in the older fields, such as mechanical. *Nevertheless,* none of the ideas given in this book are represented as being free of patents—and the author accepts no responsibility or liability from the use of any of these ideas.

Chapter 9
Making Market Research Pay Off

> ... is a popular phrase, but an ill-defined process—partly because everybody in or around marketing, sales, and advertising is an expert. This chapter gets down to basics—what market research can do, what it cannot do, how to do it, and how to evaluate what it did. It will not make you a professional MR man, but it will show you what you can expect from those who are.

WHY DO ALL THAT WORK?

Market research comes in a number of varieties—probably too many. The most elemental division is into two types. The first endeavors to obtain information or data which can aid decision making. A series of questions are posed and one of numerous research techniques is selected to obtain useful and reliable answers. These are then analyzed to obtain the information desired, which can presumably be extrapolated to represent some larger group or "universe."

The second type of research endeavors to prove something already known or claimed. In format, it is the same as the first type, although the questions are worded differently. However, the analysis technique is much different—any answers which are contrary to the point to be proven are simply thrown away. This sort of research is often used in developing statistics for advertising, distributors' presentations, lobbying, etc.

Like planning, serious market research will run contrary to the thinking of many within the firm. There are expenses and time delays involved, and these men will wonder why all this is necessary, particularly since they know the products and markets involved. Personal knowledge and opinions are useful to the firm. But when money is to be invested, facts are vital. The purpose of research is to determine these facts as accurately as possible.

There are numerous books available on market research. But for the company with no experience, it is best to work with an outside research firm, although the new-product manager must learn enough to buy these services intelligently. In every major city there are firms which specialize in market research, and these services are also available from the larger trade-magazine publishing firms, particularly McGraw-Hill and Chilton.

Both firms have done a tremendous amount of research work; not infrequently questions that arise in new-product development have already been researched. Contact these two firms before commencing any significant research. There is no point in groping for data already available. But it is done—a few years ago a major midwest steel company and one of the midwest's largest industrial advertising agencies spent (so it was reported) some $80,000 doing extensive research on advertising—specifically, readership of one-page ads versus two-page, one-color versus two-colors, etc. They derived much very useful data from this expensive project, but ironically, the same answers could have been obtained at no cost from any McGraw-Hill Publishing Co. space salesman. Before you spend a lot of money, see if the answers are already available.

TOO MANY HOLES TO THE DEN

All market research is not necessarily external—a great deal can be learned by analyzing material in the company's files: sales records, salesmens' call reports, complaint reports, etc. Market research means generating facts and indications—the source is incidental. Internal data is extremely useful when resurrecting a neglected product, marginally useful when adding a familiar product, and of almost no value when working with a completely new idea.

The less the firm knows about the product involved, the more important the research data becomes—and the more necessary it is to go outside to get the answers, obtaining the information directly from customers, prospects, or industry in general. This is usually done impersonally by mail questionnaires, which is a popular and very effective way of sampling a large audience. Or, it can be done personally, either by telephone or in face-to-face interviews, which is vastly more expensive but can generate greater depth in the data obtained. The personal interview sample is always small and requires much extrapolation. The nature of the questions and the budget available indicates which to use. Sometimes the techniques are combined, with the mail questionnaire used first for massive data, and then personal interviews to fill in the cracks and provide opinions and supplemental material.

To be effective, a mail questionnaire must be thoughtfully designed, with both your needs and the reader in mind. For instance, do not ask for specific answers in dollars or pieces when asking about current purchases—give him a selection of ranges—and a place to indicate if he does not know. Keep all questions as short and simple as possible. When practical, ask for opinions rather than facts—the reader may not be able to give an accurate answer and most respondents are almost too honest—rather than guess at numbers they will throw the questionnaire away.

Questions can be of any type—true/false, multiple choice/fill in, etc. But phrase them honestly—do not lead—and give the reader a free choice. In all multiple-choice questions, give one for "do not know," "no opinion," or "not applicable". Further, remember your audience—do not ask engineers about their firm's purchases in dollars or quantity because they will not know. Conversely, do not ask buyers technical questions. Give the man a chance to help you by asking questions which he can answer.

Length of the questionnaire ranges from 2 or 3 questions to a four-page survey that takes an hour to fill out. Each research practitioner has his own opinions about the best length. Actually the ideal length is that necessary to include a minimum number of *carefully phrased* questions. Do not try to learn everything with one mailing. Start with the broadest questions and with subsequent mailings you can become more specific. If the work is done internally, experiment with a variety of questionnaire formats and lengths until one is found which performs well for the types of research needed.

The mailing list is of extreme importance. This can be a customer list, the company's direct-mail list, a list provided by a magazine, etc. All kinds of lists are available—by industry, specific SIC groups, geographical areas, title, job function, etc. You must know the list before you can write the questions—or pick a list to match the questions. Before using your own mailing list, make certain that you know who is on it—type and size of company, geographical inequalities, title of men, etc. Most firms know next to nothing about their own lists and are better off buying or renting one.

The size of the list depends upon the size of the "universe" and desired samplings. Naturally, more respondents means more accurate answers, but printing and mailing costs are higher and tabulating and analysis costs shoot upward. So judge the number of responses needed, then make a mailing five times as great. You may get more replies than needed, but are more likely to require a supplemental mailing. If you get less than 10% response, change your list or your questionnaire.

Research can be candid or disguised. Generally, mail questionnaires are anonymous, with the reader not knowing the firm involved, and the firm cannot identify the respondent. If the mailings are personalized, with the respondent's name on the survey, repeat mailings can be made to nonrespondents in order to fill in the holes in the returns. However, the response will be light unless you also identify yourself.

Often it is important that the researcher know the identity of the respondent, but that his own identity be kept secret. Usually this occurs when each respondent represents a good prospect, and after analysis of his reply, the returned questionnaire goes to sales. If the mailing is not too large, there are all sorts of ways for secret coding of the questionnaires so that they appear to offer anonymity, but actually are identifiable when received. The process requires assigning each questionnaire to a specific name on the list and decoding it when received—a slow and expensive operation, but often well worth its costs. For mailings of less than a hundred, various versions of the questionnaire can be put on different colors of paper, one of each combination made and assigned to a specific name. One scheme involved hand trimming each sheet of paper to a slightly different size; with questionnaire versions and colored paper, this covered a mailing of nearly 1000. Another scheme involved minute pin pricks through the paper in accordance with a master numbered grid. This arrangement served for mailings of over 10,000. Such arrangements are expensive, but if the new-product manager wants to research the intended buying plans of a few thousand prospects and not only obtain statistical data but identify each respondent as well, it may be a real bargain.

Personal interview techniques, either by telephone or face-to-face, are extremely expensive and therefore limited to very small samplings. Like the mail techniques, the researcher can identify himself or be anonymous. In mail research, just print up suitable letterheads and use a blind address—somebody's aunt, your ad agency, attorney, etc. In telephone research, use direct-dial, station-to-station long distance (and you can pretend that you are calling from anywhere—New York City sounds best) and have a smooth patter for identifying your fake research firm and imaginary client. However, it has been overworked—many men researched by telephone smell a rat and are unresponsive. Nonetheless, out of 50 calls you will get cooperation from over half and the questions, if not too searching, can be quite revealing. With telephone interviews, the researcher can tailor his questions to the man's answers, thus probing more deeply or refining the questions as he goes.

The face-to-face interview is seldom used in industrial research because of its fantastic cost. The results are usually unsatisfactory because it is difficult for both parties to maintain objectivity. The only good method for keeping your own anonymity is to hire the services of research firms who specialize in such work. However, then the researchers are usually confined to a canned question routine, which loses the flexibility that is the only advantage of the personal interview. Of course, if the researcher wishes to meet his customers or prospects face-to-face to explore certain areas, this can be done. But is is financially impractical for a sampling of any significant size.

LEARNING WHAT YOU LEARNED

The hardest work is after the returns are in—analyzing the data. When working with known products, the questions can be straightforward, "Do you have a slitting line for coil metal?" But if you have a radical new-product idea, you are forced to more indirect questions—researching for needs, problems, applicability, etc. Writing the questions becomes difficult—and analysing the answers for significance is more so. Sometimes the answers and analysis seem to go nowhere. It can be that the questions do not have useful answers—or perhaps the questions are crudely phrased and do not lead the respondent to volunteer the right form of answer. All that can be done is to redesign the questionnaire and try it again.

Even when the questions and answers are useful, a great deal of careful analysis must be made, since the answers never say what you actually want to know, "Yes, I will buy your new gizmo, and do so within 90 days of your salesman's second call." Neither you nor the respondent knows that answer—he can only tell you what he knows or thinks, and it is up to you to translate that into the answers which you need.

If the questions were of the true/false or multiple-choice variety, statistical analysis will reveal "hard" data. If the questions were open, the analysis is less reliable. Further, a great deal of extrapolation is necessary—a typical project might have a 2,000-name mailing, a 20% response, and a universe of 12,000. How useful is an analysis of the 400 answers when extrapolated to cover 12,000? Of course, everything depends upon the skill of the questionnaire writer and the analyst, but that in itself is an unmeasurable factor. Every four years the American public becomes fascinated by the election predictions of the famous pollsters. Personal interviews are made, but the sampling is so tiny compared with the total electorate that it must be extrapolated almost infinitely. The pollsters fare well in some years, and poorly in others. It is a question whether such massive extrapolations are more accurate than educated guessing, random guessing, or your grandmother's Ouija board.

When useful data is vital because money will be spent on the basis of the answers, the sample must be as large as practical. Market research costs money—but mistakes cost more. Better by far to spend $10,000 researching a $1,000,000 investment than to risk it on a $500 research project.

PUTTING IT TO WORK

One warning for the neophyte new-product manager: market research, by virtue of its uncertainties, yields uncertain results. Do not hope to pin down any specific, finite answers with an accountant's accuracy. As the result of a project, you can truthfully say that 23% of the respondents said such and so. However, both you and your audience must remember the weakness of market research: the respondents might answer differently if queried a week later, the questionnaire may have repelled objective readers and attracted only the biased ones, the most important names on the list may not have answered at all—and most likely of all, the answers may involve gross distortions when extrapolated to the universe at hand. Like all statistical techniques, market research provides useful direction pointers, indicators—but not milestones or concrete measurements. It helps logical thinking men make decisions, but market research will not make the decisions for you.

Ideas Worth Exploring--No. 8

THREADING DEVICE

Description: A relatively inexpensive high-speed cutter, resembling a milling cutter except that each tooth is ground back on the front face to a different depth. The lowest tooth (which provides the shallowest cut) is used for the first pass. For the second pass, the cutter is indexed to the next tooth, which makes a somewhat deeper cut, and so on until the entire thread form has been chased. Since the stock removal per pass is relatively light, high machine speeds and feeds could be employed—yet the tool life should be excellent because of the light load per tooth.

For use on an automatic or a turret lathe, an automatic indexing device would be necessary. On an engine lathe the operator could manually index the cutter for each pass. The unit which holds the cutter could be adjustable for the different helix angles, or this might be allowed for in the cutter design.

History: A book entitled, *Shop and Foundry Practice,* Vol. 1, of a textbook by the International Correspondence School of Scranton, Pa. The issue in the author's library is the second edition, dated 1901.

Marketing Comments: Such a device could be sold by a machine-tool builder or by one which makes machine accessories. However, it would probably be more successful if marketed by a firm which works with threading tools such as taps or chasers. The market might not be great, but the tool is ideally suited for threading large-diameter work or work with a long thread. Single-point threading or thread milling is the common method, and the one shown might be superior.

Of course, the idea has application much wider than threading. It could be used for generating any deep form, particularly where close tolerances demand minimum tool wear. It appears to be an idea worth exploring. (For illustration, see following page.)

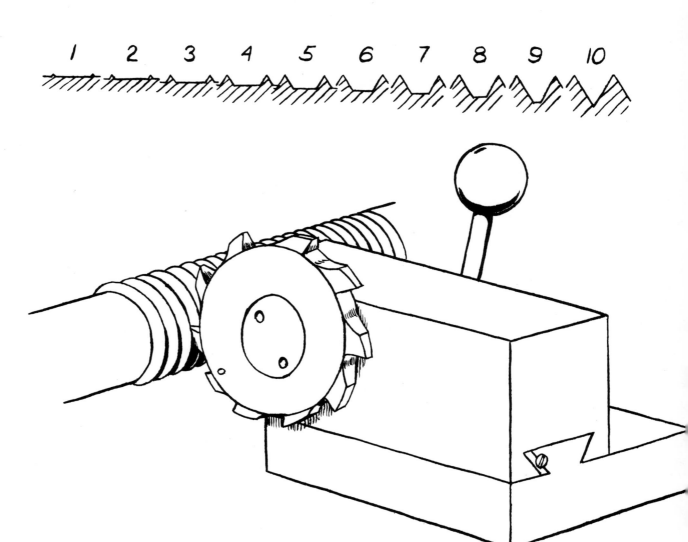

Chapter 10

How to Handle Patents

> ... legal monopolies in these days of the Federal Trade Commission and the Lea-Wheeler, Robinson-Patman, Sherman Antitrust, and Clayton Antitrust Acts. If a patent holds up in court (its mere existence is no proof that it will), it can foil competitors' plans—or foul up yours. This is an objective appraisal of the limited value of patents in today's markets—when and why to get one, how to defend it, and how to break the ones which thwart you.

HOW VALUABLE IS A PATENT?

The value of a patent is directly proportional to the size of the firm's legal staff. In bluntest terms, a patent is of little consequence if an infringer can afford to spend more money defending himself than you can spend to stop his infringement. Therefore, patents are valuable against substantially smaller competitors and dubious solace if infringed by an extremely large one.

However, intelligent management can enhance a patent's courtroom strength. If the patent is worthwhile, license it to one or more extremely large competitors. The license payment can be very modest—its existence counts, not the amount. If you need the monopoly of a patent, agreement can stipulate that the licensee will refrain from marketing the patent for a few years, giving you time to become established in the market place. But if one of the industry leaders is paying a license fee, he stamps the patent as both valid and valuable in the eyes of the court. If the patent actually does have value, your licensee should be willing to assist you in fighting off an infringer; two legal budgets are better than one.

Beyond its legal monopolistic significance, a patent means that your product has an exclusive feature, a sales point. Further, a patent has a very real psychological value—it impresses the prospect, marking your firm as a vanguard. For these reasons, the phrase "patent pending" is also a valuable marketing asset. So much so, indeed, that often it is worthwhile to apply for a patent, even when it is known that the idea is not patentable—just to be able legally to put the phrase "patent pending" upon a new product when it is introduced.

While the application is pending (which nowadays takes two years or more), no one knows what feature or aspect is covered by the application, and infringers usually hold back until they have an opportunity to examine the issued patent. Therefore, the application itself gives a measure of protection for some time. Indeed, if a patent application based upon one aspect of the design is rejected, another facet can be used for a second application. In this way, the phrase "patent pending" can be kept on a new product long enough to get ahead of impending copiers.

WHAT CAN BE PATENTED?

Any idea which displays the true spark of invention—of discovering that which was formerly unknown—can be patented. To be truly new, and patentable, the idea must not have been known in the United States, used in the United States, described in any book or magazine at any time anywhere in the world, or previously patented at any time anywhere in the world. It is difficult to be that original.

"There is no new thing under the sun"—Ecclesiastes 1:8. Except possibly for those areas at the farthest fringe of technology, this is likely to be quite true. One of the early steps, even before applying for a patent, is the patent search. Your patent attorneys attempt to find prior patents in the United States and perhaps a few leading European countries. It would be unfair to consider the average search as superficial; nonetheless, it certainly will not extend widely enough or deeply enough to cover all possible patents which might duplicate the basic concepts embodied in the application. And it is manifestly impractical for the patent attorney to search all the books and trade journals published throughout the world for the last 100 years or so. The attorney makes no attempt to do this. Therefore, a patent, even when issued, is on shaky grounds. If a competitor wishes to unseat the patent, all he need do is prove that the basic idea is not new. Any firm with the incentive to unseat a patent, and the willingness to spend money for a search through these vast mountains of paper, will probably succeed.

This vulnerability of a patent cuts both ways. If your own new-product development is blocked by a competitor's patent, send a good engineer to the library. He may be there for weeks—but it will cost less and be faster than attempting to design around the patent.

GETTING THE PATENT

There are many books available on patent practice, and every major city has patent attorneys. The new-product manager can easily learn as much as he wants to know about patents. Since the R&D head, and probably the chief engineer, will be familiar with patent-application procedures, there is no necessity for the new-product manager to dig into the subject. The only time he is likely to get involved is when he finds an idea in engineering or R&D which has new-product applicability, yet nobody else feels that the idea is significant. When this happens, make certain that the original rough sketches embodying the concept are dated and witnessed. This is vital and should be done immediately. If two or more companies should file applications for similar ideas at about the same time, that company which can prove first discovery obtains the patent.

If the original sketch is too vague to demonstrate the idea clearly, have the inventor add detail—or supplemental sketches and then write a description. You need enough notes to prove in court (perhaps many years later) the exact nature of the idea. Obtain at least two witnesses' signatures, also dated. They must be sufficiently well versed on the subject to understand the sketch and the explanation. It is best if the witnesses are outsiders, not connected with the firm.

TAKE A LOOK AT DESIGN PATENTS

The basic mechanical patent is good for 17 years and cannot be renewed. If a new-product idea represents a substantial improvement over contemporary techniques, many years may pass between the discovery of the idea and when the product assumes a secure position in the market. Often this span of years finds the company with its patents expiring just as the product is beginning to get a foothold—and become interesting to competitors. For this reason, whenever possible supplement the mechanical patent with design patents.

The subject is somewhat involved and should be discussed in detail with a patent attorney. However, at this point, any distinctive appearance of a product, or any visible component, can be protected by a design patent. The product need not necessarily be made to this appearance—that is, a given mechanical idea could be sketched up in a dozen different appearance variations and design patents obtained on each. In this way the design patents can buttress the mechanical patent and make it well-nigh impregnable.

The new-product manager might well leave basic patents up to the head of R&D and concern himself more with design patents. These offer great untapped potential.

Ideas Worth Exploring--No. 9

ROTARY ELECTRIC COUPLING

Description: Most designs for passing electrical current from a fixed member into a rotating one, such as a shaft, employ brushes and collector rings. The design is time-honored, reliable, and low in cost. However, the assembly is relatively short lived since both elements wear constantly, particularly at higher rotating speeds.

Standard tapered-roller bearings can be used for the same purpose; with the inner rings mounted on the shaft (but insulated from it) and the outer rings fixed. Current introduced to each outer ring passes through the rollers to the inner rings. The outer rings can be spring-loaded for automatic wear takeup or to maintain an established preload. Obviously, the design can be reversed—with inner ring fixed and outer rotating. One bearing is required for each wire.

Application: It is assumed that the design would often be more expensive than the familiar brush-and-collector-ring design, but it should give much longer life, particularly at elevated speeds, and thus be useful in many types of equipment, such as in machine tools. Its use would permit separate motor-driven attachments (drill speeders, etc.) on automatic screw machines, turret lathes, and other equipment. It could be used for electromagnetic face plates or lathe chucks, or for a solenoid-operated lathe chuck. The design might find wide usage in N/C machines.

Outside the tooling field, it might be suitable for certain design needs in all kinds of machinery, processing equipment, etc. It offers interesting possibilities for equipment with integral fixed-rotor electric motors.

History: The author first saw it many years ago in a developmental model for a winch. The design involved a fixed motor shaft and rotor, using the frame of a high-torque electric motor as its own cable drum.

Where to Look: The idea is almost certainly unpatented. However, a routine patent search should be made. Probably more productive would be a few days at the library, going through electrical and design engineering magazines for the past 30 or 40 years, such as *Product Engineering, Design News,* and *Electrical Design News.* Also contact the engineering departments of bearing makers.

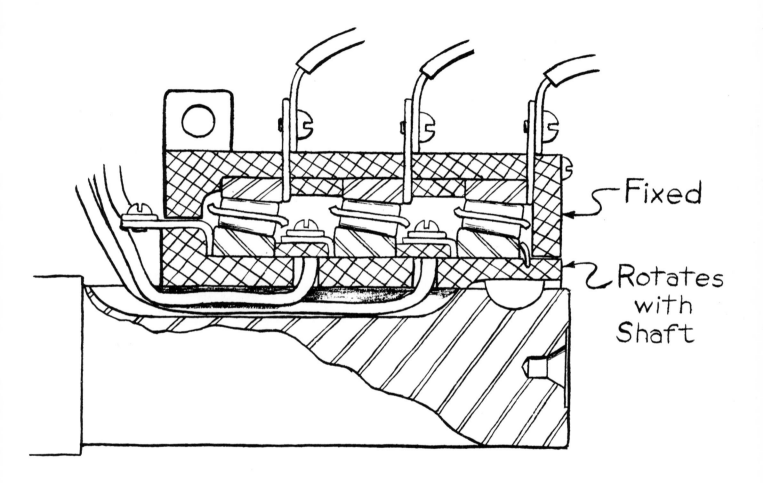

Fixed

Rotates
with
Shaft

NOTE: This is one of a number of "Ideas Worth Exploring" presented in this book. The author *has not* done this exploring. If a patent is known, it is listed. No listing does *not* mean that the idea is unpatented, or that it can be legally used in any way. Most good ideas have been patented, at one time or another. Most patents have expired and many current ones could probably be contested if literature research turned up prior exposure, as would certainly be the case with many ideas, particularly in the older fields, such as mechanical. *Nevertheless,* none of the ideas given in this book are represented as being free of patents—and the author accepts no responsibility or liability from the use of any of these ideas.

Chapter 11
Finances in New-Product Development

> . . . the proof of the pudding is in the profits—and they are in the future. Like the farmer, in new-product development you plant investments today and hope to reap profits in the fall. For this reason, financial people tend to turn a less-than-enthusiastic eye upon new-product financial projections. Here is how to get them involved, to employ their expertise rather than fight it, and how to assure yourself that your profit projections are, indeed, sound.

WHAT WILL IT COST?

Many elements of the new-product cost are established by the design. It should be tailored to the volume expected for the first two years or so, and design changes should have been planned to occur as volume passes certain levels. These design changes, plus corresponding changes in production methods and tooling and a drop in cost of most purchased components (quantity prices and also design shifts), produce steady decreases in total cost as the volume mounts.

All too often a product is engineered and designed, then presented as a *fait accompli* to those who will design the tooling. This must be avoided, since most of the dimensions and tolerances applied are more or less empiric and can be deliberately established to ease manufacturing. Throughout this product/tool-design phase, watch for individuals with narrow experience—men who prefer metal to plastics, for example—merely because they know the former and are unfamiliar with the latter. Insular thinking of this kind will always increase the product costs, because decisions are made on the basis of that which is comfortable, rather than that which is best.

With product engineering and tool engineering in agreement as to methods, the tooling requirements are readily estimated and direct labor costs predicted. This normally poses no problem, except where unfamiliar machines and methods are employed. In this case, vendor estimates must be relied upon, although occasionally these can be checked by getting quotations on the same work from outside suppliers.

More troublesome are operations in assembly, inspection, packaging, etc., since these are manual—difficult to predict because they rely on level of skill required and available, productivity, layout of worksite, and similar variables. An educated guess has to suffice unless an experienced time-and-motion man is available, who will then give you *his* educated guess.

Adding the total labor cost (bearing in mind a reasonable scrap and rework expectation), to the cost of purchased materials, components and services, yields the total net cost. This should be compared with that for other company products which may be similar, as a double check and to find the normal relationship between cost and selling price. Determine what percentage of the gross profit goes for administrative, sales, and other overhead elements and add this to the net cost of the new product to arrive at the accounting cost.

The biggest danger is when the company's internal cost system is obsolete, inaccurate, or does not exist. When this occurs (which is often) the relationship between net cost and gross profit (overhead + net profit) is unrealistic—usually with net costs shown lower than they actually are. This means that the overhead percentage is shown on the books higher than it actually is, and if the same percentage is applied to the estimated net cost of the new product, an unreasonably high total cost results. Make certain that new-product costing is not burdened by such internal record deficiencies. Analyze the projected total cost to see if it is reasonable, comparing the resultant selling price against that for comparable products sold to the same market.

WHAT WILL IT SELL FOR?

Adding total cost, profit, and distribution markups automatically produces the selling price. However, this may not be the optimum price for a new product. If the product is similar to those now sold by others, establish the selling price a few percent less than competitors' prices. It is a nice "irritant" factor and gives the salesmen a talking point.

If the product is unique—differs substantially from competitive offerings—the design or production methods might permit a much lower price than competitive equivalents. Beware—most customers distrust too-low prices, equating them with poor quality. Besides, if the product is sold substantially below competitors' prices, you apply too much pressure, forcing them to develop a similar product or strengthen their sales efforts. Further, you do not want to lose the opportunity for an unusually high profit.

If a price higher than equivalent products is visualized, it poses problems. It may be justified if sales features and quality warrant it, but quality at a price is hard to sell. If the product has little repeat potential, customers will do a lot of analysis before paying the higher price for a supposedly superior product. And if the product is consumed (supplies, components, etc.) buying is done on price/cost—and attempting to sell quality at a higher price may be fruitless.

If the product is dramatically new—not at all comparable with anything now available—the selling price requires careful thought, since it is not necessarily a function of the cost. However, nothing exists in a vacuum—everything has some worth, and an idea of what this should be can be gained by comparing the product and its customer benefits with the products or methods which it displaces. The more advanced the new product, the more attractive its selling points and price must be to entice customers into something completely new.

A high profit in the initial stages is desirable because it permits rapid return on development and tooling costs and self-finances rapid inventory build-up. However, if careful analysis by outsiders would reveal this high profit, it may attract competition too rapidly. On the other hand, a lower price makes the product less attractive to competition—but to your own firm, also. Probably the best rule of thumb is to start out at the highest price attractive to customers, with full expectation of reducing it as soon as competition appears. In any case, the pricing of a completely new product requires a great deal of finesse. Sometimes market research can feel out price reactions. Occasionally a firm makes trial sales, before the selling price is established at all. From this, the customer reaction to the product itself and its price is determined—which may be useful in arriving at the final selling price.

CRYSTAL-BALLING THE VOLUME

The financial attractiveness of a new product is determined by the investment required, the profit to be made, and the relative timing of the two. Generally, much of the investment occurs before the product even appears on the market. Obviously, the profits come only after a substantial number of units have been sold. Thus, while the investment timing is largely fixed, the profit timing tends to be quite vague. It all depends upon the sales volume.

The new-product manager will have a sales forecast which he feels can be accomplished by some future time, 3 or 5 years away. But in predicting the volume between the first day and that future point, problems arise. One man will draw a straight line, giving a linear annual growth between the two points. Another will assume a rapid initial growth and then a tapering off. A third will draw the curve the other way, with a slow growth rate the first year or so, then gradually accelerating until by the nth year, sales are climbing rapidly. For every product, one of these is realistic—but none of them can be proven.

How to predict sales volume was covered in Chapter 5. Matching lists of known prospects, extrapolating this to cover unknown prospects in similar SIC categories, determining a sales goal for each firm, assigning the prospects to the salesmen, and then predicting the penetration for each year—all this is time-consuming and frustrating guesswork. It makes both the new-product manager and the sales manager realize how little they know about their own salesmen and their prospects, and just how unpredictable selling can be. However, from an accumulation of small individual guesses comes a reasonably accurate overall estimate, a realistic projection which is vastly better than a pure guess or wishful thinking.

MAKE VERSUS BUY

Although inside-versus-outside decisions are made at every level of new-product development—including tooling, components, subassemblies, perhaps the entire product—even then such decisions are frequently not given the thought they deserve. Particularly so when it involves buying the entire new product from outside—or buying a firm which manufactures a similar product, and putting the new product through their production facilities.

It is difficult to generalize, but the new-product manager must remember that there are many alternates, and each should be analyzed before automatically assuming that the product will be made internally. External manufacture of subassemblies is common. And external manufacture of the complete new product might be wise if the firm's own facilities are loaded, if the product requires a drastically different form of experience and methods, or if the quality involved is either much better or lower than that with which the firm's production employees are familiar.

For instance, if the firm's products require precise machining and assembly, then a simple welded new product should probably be purchased outside. If the firm is in metalworking and the new product is mostly plastic, it might be wise to farm it out. The long-term objective would probably be to bring the product back in. However, during the stages of debugging, tooling, and minor redesign, much strain can be avoided by working with outsiders who are experienced with the materials and methods involved.

END OF THE RAINBOW

In predicting profits from a new product, remember that it must pay for many things—development expenses, inventory investment, purchased capital equipment, tooling, sales expenses, and a host of other things. The cost of materials, labor, components, overhead, and routine sales and promotion are part of the total cost of the product. However, abnormal costs and all investments come from profits. Therefore, the profits generated by a new product should be used to break even and for bootstrapping—lifting the product into higher sales volume and higher profit areas. When or before the new product has paid off the original investment, it will have achieved a sales volume that means redesign and different production methods in order to broaden the profit. In turn, this requires new tooling, and reinvestment. Furthermore, the new-product manager must assume that the product will attract competition which may force price reductions and a narrower margin. Competition often forces reinvestment in advanced facilities—not for higher profits, but merely to retain part of the original profit.

The point is that during its first years, a new product is likely to be profitless, in the sense that while the product does make money, it reabsorbs it all in financing its own growth. After the first two or three years, the product should not *cost* the company anything—but it is unlikely to contribute any significant net profit to the firm. A belated realization of this fact dampens the enthusiasm of men who have struggled for two or three years to bring a new product to marketing success. However, it is a fact of life and should be anticipated in advance, rather than discovered at leisure. No product yields a profit during its adolescent, fast-growth years. Only when the sales curves start to level off does its profit exceed its own needs.

Ideas Worth Exploring—No. 10

VERTICAL SHAPER/BROACH

Description: The machine combines the principles of the familiar shaper and the vertical surface-broaching machine. The vise head moves into the cutting tool (rather than crosswise), as the ram makes a predetermined number of cutting strokes, so that an extremely short surface broach could be used for heavy stock removal. The concept could be employed in machines ranging from simple tool-room units to completely automatic ones for production applications.

In operation, the workpiece would be clamped in the vise and advanced to the starting position. The ram descends, making the first pass. The work-holding head retracts a few thousandths while the ram returns to its upper position, and then advances for the second pass. By automatic cycling, the work could be advanced between strokes to the full depth required to broach the finished shape.

History: A doodle of the author's, based loosely on a combination of machine-tool elements and a device used by my grandmother to make sauerkraut.

Marketing Comments: The maximum depth of cut per inch of broach length is rather limited—averaging perhaps 0.002 for tough steel. Thus, a form requiring a 1/2 in. depth of cut would require some 250 inches of working broach length. For this reason, broaching is largely limited to applications requiring modest depth of cut. However, the machine described could provide that 1/2-inch deep cut with only 25 inches of working length, taking ten strokes to complete the work.

The concept might advance broaching into many applications where it is now denied because of the high machine-tool investment and the cost of the broaching tools when deep cuts are involved. If developed successfully—either at the tool-room or production-machine levels—marketing potential might be considerable.

For illustration, see following page.

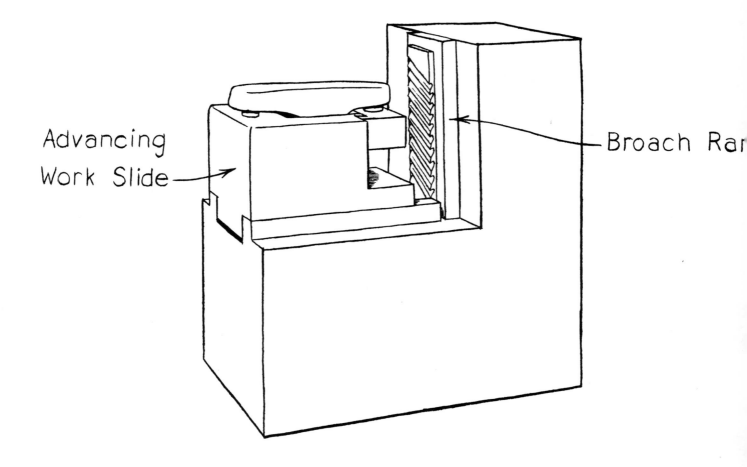

Advancing Work Slide

Broach Rar

NOTE: This is one of a number of "Ideas Worth Exploring" presented in this book. The author *has not* done this exploring. If a patent is known, it is listed. No listing does *not* mean that the idea is unpatented, or that it can be legally used in any way. Most good ideas have been patented, at one time or another. Most patents have expired and many current ones could probably be contested if literature research turned up prior exposure, as would certainly be the case with many ideas, particularly in the older fields, such as mechanical. *Nevertheless,* none of the ideas given in this book are represented as being free of patents—and the author accepts no responsibility or liability from the use of any of these ideas.

Chapter 12
The Contribution of Engineering to Profitable New Products

> ... the design of a new product is of vital importance—it affects its cost, quality, producibility, and salability. So a smoothly working relationship with engineering is indispensable. This chapter tells how to work around a recalcitrant engineering department, and (in a happier climate) how to obtain the best efforts of your firm's engineers. In particular, it stresses the importance of a flexible approach to design, the vital necessity of a smooth interface between engineering and production, and how to see that the product is tailored for lowest cost at different volume levels.

INSIDE VERSUS OUTSIDE

A great deal of new-product design engineering can be purchased from outside specialists. Such firms work at a wide range of levels—mere drafting-board supplements to the internal staff, specialists in certain areas which may be unfamiliar, perhaps a contract with some noncompetitive firm who has a great deal of experience in the area, industrial designers (who specialize in appearance, convenience, and salability), and firms who provide the complete package—research, development, design and engineering. The last are capable of taking the concept from feasibility research to the market stage.

The decisions concerning outside engineering are based upon company policy, how related the new product is to the firm's present products, whether engineering is capable of doing the job, workload of the engineering staff, and sometimes the cooperation of the engineering department. Thus, design engineering becomes another function which the new-product manager can acquire outside if the internal group is disinterested or incompetent.

There are advantages to buying engineering outside. Among these is adherence to a precommitted budget. Due to their extremely wide range of experience, outside firms often provide more sophisticated engineering concepts than the internal engineering department. These firms usually have industrial designers on their staff and the end result can be a much more attractive package (and quite frequently a lower-cost unit) than if internally designed.

However, all is not rosy. External development and engineering costs are high. Further, if the engineering is done outside, then the company engineers are not intimately familiar with the design, resent it, and tend to nit-pick it. When it comes time to develop larger or smaller models or redesign for changes in product volume, the outside design may become a problem. Another weak point is that internal development involves cooperation between R&D, engineering, tool engineering, and production—and often foresees and avoids problem areas. An outside firm, not benefiting from the informal note-matching that goes on internally, is more likely to run afoul of tooling or production difficulties, simply because these departments were excluded from design decisions.

REDESIGN IN ADVANCE

While it has been mentioned before, it cannot be overstressed—both design and tooling are a function of production volume. In the initial stages of the new product, it should be designed and tooled for modest production rates. It is suicidal to freeze a design requiring high-production tooling when sales do not warrant it. If this occurs, the firm is locked into excessively high inventories and the entire cost structure is unrealistic. Designing each component part and its tooling for each of a number of production levels can become quite complex, but it is extremely vital and much too often forgotten; a direct if seldom-traveled route to high profits. In American industry, it is not at all unusual to find a part being manufactured in the same manner as was done in its initial stages, although production volume has long since passed the point when a major redesign and shift to higher production methods should have been adopted.

A direct benefit of deliberately planning redesign and tooling changes in advance is that tool engineering take a more realistic approach. If they know that the tooling is for the initial stages only, and has a useful life of perhaps one year, they develop different designs than when the tooling will be used for an indefinite time.

DESIGN VERSUS TOOLING

It is vitally important that tool engineering meet with design engineering at the very earliest stage of design development. The more usual procedure is for design engineering to assume a know-it-all attitude and develop the design independently, freeze it into engineering drawings, and then pass it along to tool engineering as a sort of hot potato. When the tooling is developed, refinements or simplification of the design often become desirable, and problems and delays occur as tool engineering goes back to design engineering for a redesign of first one component and then another. It is better by far to have these two departments work together.

Cooperation at this level eliminates some of the perennial aggravation of manufacturing—unrealistic tolerances, meaningless surface finishes, parts that are hard to hold, features that are difficult to inspect, etc. Ideally, the new-product manager will have a production background—at least being able to look at design engineering's work through tooling's viewpoint—and vice versa. If he can do this, he can arbitrate disputes and speed up the entire project. If he has no production experience, the more quickly he becomes familiar with design and tooling concepts, the better off he will be.

THE PROTOTYPE

It will be necessary to build a prototype—perhaps many of them. Even if the new product is an extremely expensive machine, a prototype is necessary—if only to show to potential customers, to top management for approval, and to debug the design concepts. If the product is relatively inexpensive, a number of prototypes should be made, since these can be used in field testing.

The prototypes should be, as nearly as possible, faithful reproductions of the actual product. In many cases, those incorporating components suitable only to high production (injection-molded plastics, die castings, stampings, etc.), this may be difficult to achieve. For instance, zinc die castings could not be used in a prototype unit but duplicates might be machined from aluminum or made from some substitute material such as a low-temperature alloy. Cast plastic parts can be used to duplicate molded parts, etc.

The closer the prototype resembles the production unit, the more valuable it becomes. Accurate prototypes are very useful in visualizing tooling requirements, planning assembly operations, inspection techniques, packaging, and for other in-plant considerations. Further, they are more valuable for gaining management approval, customer reaction, for training the sales force, and for advertising purposes. They are indispensable for meaningful field testing. It is self-evident that the field-tested prototype must duplicate the actual production model if results of the field tests are to be applicable.

Thus the prototype, in spite of its disproportionate cost, is indispensable and should be approached with the full intention of making it as accurate a rendition of the production unit as possible.

Ideas Worth Exploring--No. 11

PIERCING ROLLS FOR FORMING MACHINE

Description: Two geared rolls (the die roll substantially larger diameter than the punch roll) are driven by the final station of a roll-forming machine so that the piercing rolls have the same surface speed as the moving strip. The rolls contain mated punches and die buttons to suit the workpiece. Dies are standard, but the punches have a relief behind the cutting edge; their life would be short—only one or two sharpenings.

The piercing action is generated—the punch contacts the workstrip at an angle and rolls into it; slug separation occurs about at the centerline. The punch rolls out of the pierced hole as the strip passes; greater relief might be desirable on this side of the punch to avoid making an elongated hole.

If the workpiece is relatively short (not greater than the circumference of a reasonable-sized punch roll), shearing die sections could be incorporated for cutoff. This would eliminate the conventional flying shear and assure both accurate length and register of the holes in relation to the ends of the stock.

History: A 20-year old design of the author's used successfully on 20-guage cold-rolled steel strip.

Marketing Comments: The design could be marketed by a firm selling roll-forming machines, interchangeable punches and dies, or punch and die components. Overall cost of roll piercing tools should not be greater than for a comparable piercing die—and the labor and machine-cost savings would more than offset the greater punch cost of the roll tools. While applications would be limited to volume operations, roll-forming itself is a high-production method. The total market potential could be quite high.

Spinoff Ideas: The idea might be practical on a coil-fed punch press, to do some of the piercing outside the die. In progressive dies, this also might eliminate the one or two die stations taken up for piercing the index notches.

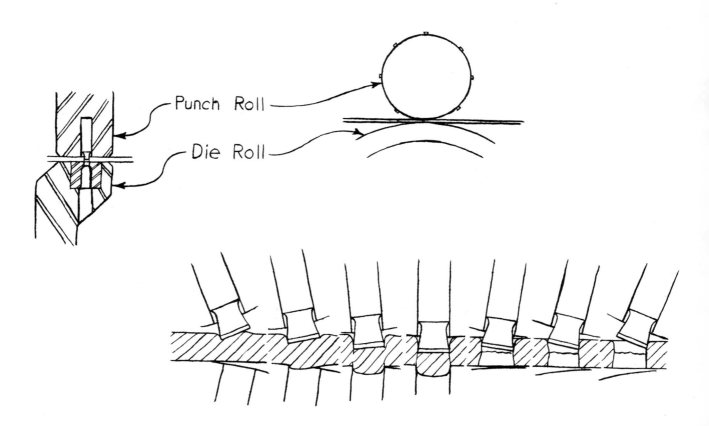

Punch Roll

Die Roll

Chapter 13

Getting Into Production

> ... product design, methods engineering, and production blend in well-managed new-product development. Since new products often involve production methods that are also new to the firm, the product and its facilities may need to be developed together. One of the two biggest traps for new products is bumbling during initial production runs. Here is how to avoid problems and achieve a smooth, well-organized transition between idea and actuality.

FIRST THINGS FIRST

Tool design is a very involved field. In its widest and usual sense, it includes establishing the sequence of operations and manufacturing tolerances, the production methods, machines, tools, dies, jigs and fixtures for holding the work and guiding the tool, inspection procedures and equipment, etc. If all this is done ingeniously and professionally, the product is manufactured satisfactorily and at the lowest practical cost. If tool design is less than the best, product quality suffers, scrap is abnormal and costs are out of line.

Further, the new-product manager should see that the jigs and fixtures are designed and made in the proper order, starting with the first operation. Too frequently tool engineers take the most challenging (or sometimes the easiest) operation and design the jigs and fixtures for it, then work in both directions. This is wrong. The correct way is to start at operation No. 1, establish tolerances, and then design the jigs and fixtures for it. Operation No. 2 follows, and so on. When a logical progression is not followed, tooling for one operation is designed based upon assumed specifications from some previous operation. But when the tooling for that operation is designed, the specifications are likely to change, which makes tooling designs for subsequent operations obsolete. Even if the new-product manager is not a production expert, he can at least watch for the fundamentals of good practice.

SEEING IF IT WORKS

The product has been proven, by mock-ups when necessary. But in the interchange of ideas between product engineering, tool engineering, and production, design details of the product are altered, sometimes drastically. If these changes affect the functioning of the product, it may be necessary to reprove the design.

The tooling may also incorporate untried concepts. These too should be made in mock-up form and proven. The new-product manager can uncover tooling problems by looking critically and listening carefully. If the tooling is not right, others will have noticed it, and there will be low-voiced grumblings which the new-product manager must tune in on.

With existing products, deficient tooling can be patched up and the repair costs buried. But with a new product, every penny will show up. Since the new-product manager has told management what this tooling will cost, it is important to him to see that it stays within the budget. This is best accomplished by making certain that the tooling design is fundamentally sound, that any tricky ideas are proven in advance, and that critical voices are listened to.

GETTING TO WORK

After top management approves swinging into full production, materials and components are brought in, the new tooling goes onto the machines, and actual production commences. This, of course, is the acid test—everything works well or it seems that nothing at all does. Manufacturing is an endless series of snags; many of them are expected, but others become outright emergencies. In new-product production, if anything can go wrong, it will. The wise new-product manager will have included slack in his lead-time estimate and in his budget, for ironing out petty problems. It is almost certain to be necessary.

LOADING THE SHELVES

In every kind of new product except those which are custom designed for specific customer's needs, an initial inventory is an absolute must. These products must be carefully checked out for quality and proper functioning. Initial impressions are lasting; if the first customers are disappointed by early shipments, they sour both the distributors and the salesmen. Gradually debugging the product over the first few months of production is suicidal. Instead, set inspection at its most critical level. Nothing that deviates from the print is "good enough." Later, when the new product settles into routine production, many inspection procedures can be relaxed or eliminated. But during the first six months or so, inspect everything.

All too often, the initial production runs are faulty. These must be scrapped and replaced, or go back for expensive rework. Inventory schedules are fouled up, the product introduction must be held off (if possible), and the master plan, scheduling, and budgets all go askew. So above all else, insist upon an extremely high quality-control level for every production operation on the first few runs. It will pay off handsomely.

Initial production is for the preliminary stock requirements. This production run should be made leisurely, allowing adequate time for delivery of material and components, for the abnormally high quality-control required, for debugging, and for unforeseen problems that are bound to arise. Quantities and sizes for the initial inventory have been decided in advance. Generally, this should be a rather large inventory, since it is impossible to accurately predict which sizes will be the most popular. If in doubt, overstock. The cost is less than that of lost sales if the inventory is inadequate.

When the initial run has been finished, and everyone is satisfied that it is complete and the products are good and salable, then the next production runs are made in accordance with the anticipated sales volume for the first few months, with the initial inventory becoming the "float." This is contrary to normal practice. Usually the initial inventory is as small as humanly possible and subsequent production runs are made grudgingly, just enough to cover purchase orders actually received. This penny-wise and pound-foolish policy avoids investing in a slow-moving inventory (after investing many times as much in development and initial sales costs)—but it also means low quality as individual orders are rushed through to fill an order, poor delivery at the worst possible time, and frustrated distributors and salesmen. With typical management, a few dollars can be saved on the initial inventory—and thousands lost. This can spell a premature end for a new product that was carefully developed in every other respect.

WHEN DOES THE CURTAIN GO UP?

Sales activities commence only *after* the initial product inventory is finished, inspected, and on the shelf—and not before. Under no circumstances should sales calls be made until the product is ready for immediate shipment. Of all new-product failures, the most common is where production and sales started at the same time, so the first customers were forced to wait, and orders were cancelled or buyers complained bitterly about delivery. The salesmen and distributors who grab the ball and run with it (the most valuable ones for new-product development) discover that the ball does not really exist. Ultimately, six months or so later, all the production and inventory problems are smoothed out and the product is ready to go. But then it is too late. With salesmen and distributors, once burned is very definitely twice warned. These men make their living by pleasing customers, not aggravating them. They want no part of a new product which will make enemies—or lose good customers for other products. Before the sales department heads for the bush, make absolutely certain that the bird is in hand.

Ideas Worth Exploring--No. 12

DRAWER SUSPENSION DESIGN

Description: A simple concept, involving hinged members between the end of a drawer and the inside back of the cabinet. The drawer end would have to be engineered to accommodate the loading imposed. However, the device supports a drawer when completely extended, without the necessity for expensive and space-consuming telescoping suspension systems.

The design could be as accurate and/or strong as necessary—to accommodate any level of precision or loading required for the drawer and its contents. Applications could range from furniture through electronic chassis. As shown, the design serves a drawer with movement equal to twice its width; additional plates in the hinge permit longer travel.

History: Developed in the mid '50s for an automotive accessory—an under-the-dash drawer for miscellaneous objects. The design provided full extension of the drawer and performed quite satisfactorily.

Marketing Comments: Either a product, or an interesting design refinement which might greatly reduce the cost of certain types of furniture, office equipment, and electronic cabinets, particularly where the loading is heavy.

Where to Look: A simple application of an ancient idea. It would not be patentable.

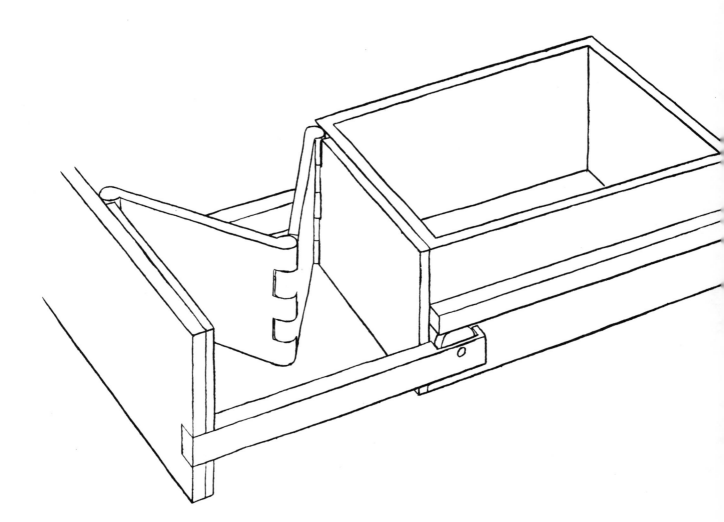

Chapter 14

Promoting the New Product

> . . . an introduction to how to promote and advertise a new product—which is often vastly different from how an older, established product is advertised. Here are the working tools for introducing the new product, finding valid prospects, and even for selling. While the new-product manager need not be an expert in this field, he cannot escape the necessity of judging others' programs—and that means knowing what promotion tool to use when, how to use it, and what to expect from it.

THE PURSE STRINGS

There is one certain fact in advertising: that the best way to waste an advertising investment is to make it too small. Someone in the company will know the percentage of sales volume invested in advertising. Usually this is a ridiculously small amount, often less than 1%. Attempts will be made to fit the new product into this standard budget. It cannot be done, unless much of the routine advertising is suspended. The only logical way to draw up a budget for a new product is on the "task" basis.

Find the company's present cost per inquiry, and the percentage of inquiries which become customers. This gives the dollars of promotional pressure required to find a prospect and convert him to a customer. Played against the new-product sales forecast, it gives a reasonable advertising budget. But the resultant figure will probably be astronomical—do not expect management to approve it. Nonetheless, it is a guide, and the argument may be convenient in selling the budget.

When preparing the proposed advertising budget, be certain to allow a large percent for contingencies—10 to 20% of the budget. A new product often provides promotion opportunities which cannot be forecast. For instance, early sales may provide material for case-histories. While this can be anticipated, case-history costs are difficult to predict—and an unusually good one may be worth promoting more heavily than anticipated. Often there are opportunities for demonstrating the new product at private trade shows put on by distributors. At major trade shows you may get exhibitors of complementary products to show your product with theirs. Such opportunities are difficult to predict and must be financed from the "contingencies" category. Therefore, when the budget is firmed up make the contingencies box as large as possible.

After years of working at it, the author still does not know how to convince top management of the benefits of industrial advertising. This problem is common in advertising circles and fosters phrases such as, "He does (or does not) believe in advertising," as though advertising was an obscure religion, to be accepted on faith alone. Unfortunately, about all that can be proven is that companies who advertise heavily and consistently grow and make money, while those which do little advertising are often on the downhill run. However, it does not necessarily prove that advertising makes the difference—merely that progressive managements advertise more heavily than those who are complacent or tired.

PUBLICITY

This often unexploited promotion tool offers valuable opportunities for a new product. Editors are willing to publish useful and interesting information about anything which is not common industry practice. The cost of publicity is very low, only that of preparing the material; magazines do not charge for publishing publicity. Unfortunately, your advertising manager may be of little help, since many are aware of publicity but extremely inexperienced in its use.

There are a number of different types of publicity: releases for new products and literature, short nonexclusive picture stories, exclusive case-history articles, exclusive technical articles, and various types of announcements.

The new-product release is a factual one-page (double-spaced) description of the product, its application, and technical features. It should be accompanied by a 4 x 5 inch photograph. If the product, such as a chemical, cannot be illustrated, include a pertinent chart, graph, schematic, microphotograph, etc. Send the release to every magazine which conceivably might be interested in it. The average release is mailed to 25 or 30 magazines. But there are over 3000 trade and specialty magazines; a new-product manager reaching for the broadest possible market could probably find 250 or 300 which might be interested. The objective is to obtain inquiries—the more places the release appears, the more inquiries it will produce.

The literature release announces the availability of new literature, but the description in the release is of the product, although it is logical to commence by saying that "product X is described in a new four-page two-color brochure." Always mail a copy of the brochure with the release because having it in the editor's file may help get the product included in round-up articles. Again, make the mailing as widespread as possible.

The nonexclusive short article is brief, two-or-three pages (double-spaced), usually (but not always) a case-history describing a typical or unusual application, and illustrated by two or three good photos. They are easy to write and popular with advertising agencies because they impress management. However, they are seldom worthwhile, just because they are nonexclusive—very few leading editors will even consider such material, since their competition might be publishing the same item.

The exclusive case-history article and the *exclusive technical article* are offered to only one magazine; if this magazine rejects the article, it may be offered to the second-choice magazine, and so on. However, the article *must* be exclusive. The case-history article is a description of how the product is used in an unusual or extremely successful way, and the results obtained. Where it can be done in a nonderogatory fashion, describe before and after to drive home the point. Generally, a case-history article is relatively short—four to eight manuscript pages, and liberally illustrated.

In the course of editing, the editor will remove any puff or obvious sales pitch—unless you do a good job of writing. The best way to keep your sales features in the article is to build the story upon them. For instance, if the primary sales features of the product are high speed and rigidity, then the article should give the advantages of high speed, how this capability was achieved, and how the customer benefits—particularly as compared with the low speeds which he formerly employed. If rigidity is important, discuss the problems caused by lack of rigidity and how the product solved them.

Case-history articles are valuable publicity for two reasons. First, they show the product actually in use—prospects reading the article become more interested when they see that someone else is profiting from the product. Second, they can be turned out in volume—it is not at all difficult to generate a dozen or more worthwhile case-history articles each year. However, remember that each case-history must be gathered with the permission and cooperation of the customer involved, working with his advertising or public relations department and obtaining their approval. Think before you include the customer's name. To do so implies his recommendation, complicates getting his approval, and is a road map for competitors. Conversely, the customer may want his name mentioned—since then the article is publicity for him too.

The technical article is handled similarly, except that it can be considerably longer—if the article subject is of fairly broad interest and there is enough meat to warrant it, a manuscript might run 12 or more pages in length. It should be as well illustrated as possible.

Typical subjects include how to select. ., how to apply . ., troubleshooting, design of accessories, etc. An analysis of a few trade magazines will show the nature of a typical technical article.

While a case-history article often has no byline (author's name), the technical article always should have one. The title is the important point—the best ones are chief engineer, service engineer, production engineer, tool engineer, field engineer, etc. If for promotional purposes you want the article bylined by one of the salesmen, do not use that title—use field engineer, or application engineer. If your chief engineer never leaves the plant, do not put his name on the article—use someone who contacts customers. A good technical article is a prestige-building device—use it to best advantage. But have the man read the article before it appears in print—all sorts of embarrassing situations arise if this is forgotten.

ADVERTISING

No one company's advertising experience is broad enough to encompass all types of advertising and advertising concepts. There are two different types of ads in new-product promotion. Oversimplified, they are the full or half-page high readership ad, and the smaller high-inquiry ad. The two go into different types of magazines. The only practical way to develop ads of maximum effectiveness is to go to one or two of the leading magazines in the market involved and discuss the problem with them. If you are not familiar with it, obtain a copy of McGraw-Hill's research, *Laboratory of Advertising Performance*. A thoughtful study of this material will teach you more about the mechanics of successful advertising than most professional ad men know. Suggesting that you put this vast pool of knowledge and experience to work is the best possible advice.

Usually, publishers can provide marked-up copies of pertinent magazines, showing the readership and inquiries produced by each ad. Obviously, search for common factors of appearance, presentation, and tone among the successful ads, and emulate them.

There are various readership-interview techniques and measurements, but most follow the lead of the Starch studies, giving two or three scores: "Noted"—which means the reader remembered seeing the ad (and that's all he remembered); "Seen Associated"—he remembered the ad and connected it with the company name; and "Read Most" (which means that he read half or more of the words in the ad). Of these three scores, the only one of any practical value is the "Read Most," where the prospect saw the ad, had it catch his attention, and then found it interesting enough to read half or more of the copy. Study the ads with high "Read Most" scores. Almost without exception they will have interesting and pertinent illustrations, an arresting headline, and straightforward, factual copy.

DIRECT MAIL

If you are selling extremely expensive capital equipment, a direct-mail campaign will not produce purchase orders. But most firms completely overlook the fact that direct mail can produce purchase orders for lower-priced items and opportunities to quote on high-ticket products. Unfortunately, experts at industrial direct mail are hard to find. Most agencies and direct-mail houses are intensely "creative." This may produce a very productive campaign. Equally often, it produces a very expensive campaign of negligible value. The best rule is the same as with advertising: keep the promotion attractive, factual, informative, and medium pressure. Give the reader solid reasons to become interested, and tell him why he should order a unit for trial or return the card or form to obtain additional information or to have your salesmen call. Know exactly what you want your direct mail campaign to accomplish and then design it to meet this objective.

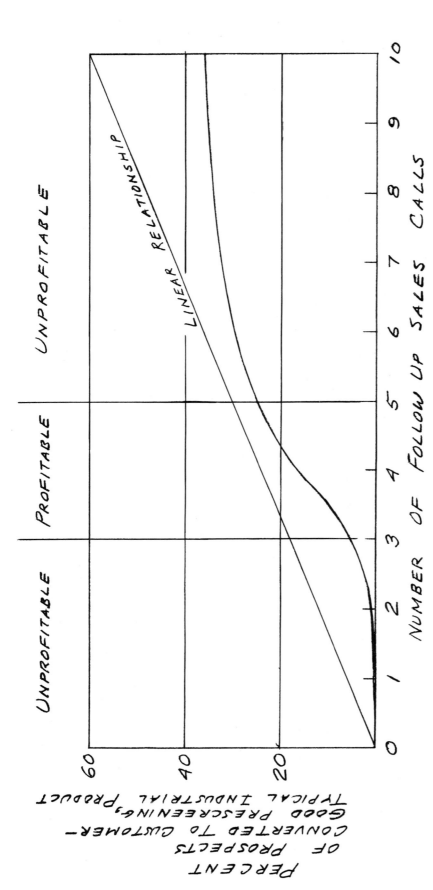

Figure 14-1A

Sales build up from repeat sales calls. Notice that one-shot sales calls are a waste of time; two calls are better; but it takes three calls to convert enough prospects into customers to make the process profitable. However, perseverance has its limitations. Productivity after the sixth call drops off too rapidly to be worthwhile.

This presupposes, of course, that the prospect *is* a prospect—that he has been prescreened and correctly evaluated. If not, then consider the first call a prescreening call, rather than a sales call.

Currently, a manufacturer's sales call costs $58.98 (McGraw-Hill Research Laboratory of Advertising Performance). Cutting off at 5 calls on each prospect, 25 out of 100 will have become customers—after an investment in 376 sales calls of $22,176 or $887 per customer obtained. At 8% after-tax profit, the break-even volume per new customer is $11,088!

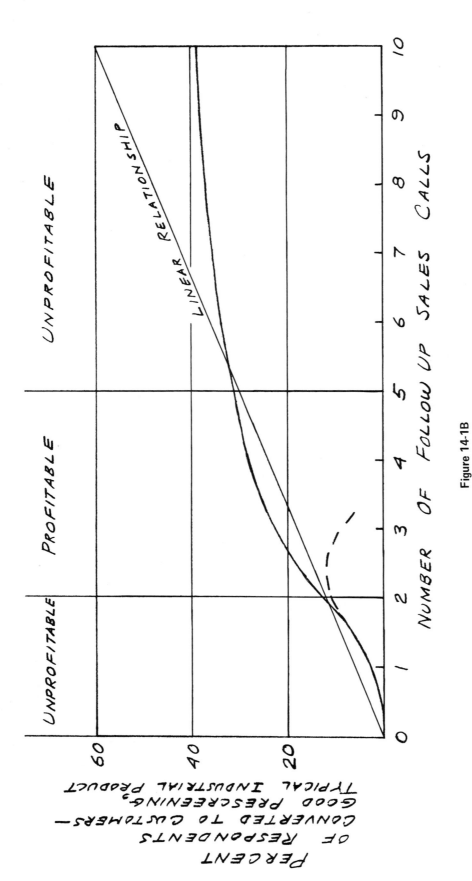

Figure 14-1B

Sales come faster if the salesman is following a bona-fide inquiry. If complete literature and price information are mailed to the prospect, he may even reach an order before the salesman reaches him. But experience indicates that the unprofitable point still occurs at about the sixth followup. Stopping after the fifth call on each remaining prospect, 32 of 100 are customers—after an investment in 333 calls of $19,640 or $614 per customer. The break-even volume on each one is $7672.

Notice the dash line—it represents people who buy when they should not, because either they or the salesmen made an error in judging the fit between product and need. If the customer orders a product which he cannot use, he may return it and he may not. But if the salesman sells something which the customer cannot use, he is almost certain to return it.

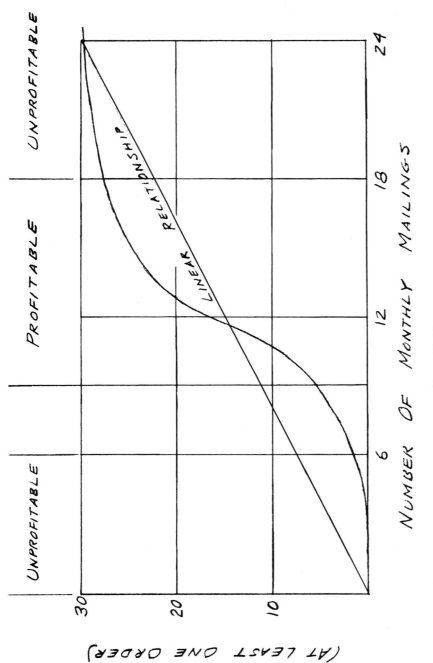

Figure 14-1C

Sales from direct-mail promotion of industrial products. This is an accurate plot, based upon long-term experience with a number of disposable products purchased by manufacturing firms throughout the U.S. and Canada. The mailing lists were formed from names of men who responded to magazine advertising and publicity, letters, phone inquiries, and other initial contacts by the prospect.

All the products were sold exclusively by mail—no salesmen or agents—using steady monthly mailings of factual promotion material, complete with prices. Competition ranged from low to moderate; average initial sale for all products was about $75 (range of $35 to $800). The campaign materials and lists were constantly refined; over a number of years of experience, it was found that 24 mailings provided the maximum obtainable value from each name. Notice that direct mail takes four to five times as long to secure the initial order as does a salesman and that it is about 1/3 less effective in converting prospects into customers.

Each name receives 24 mailings. At a high average of 50 cents each, there are 2400 mailings per 100 prospects: $1200. A good campaign will produce 29 customers at the end of two years, at an average cost of $41.38, and a break-even volume of $517 each.

181

The real secret of direct-mail success is the same as in personal selling—perseverance. Figures 14-1A, 14-1B, and 14-1C show the amount of work required to make a sale; it takes time and persistency. A one-shot mailing is a waste of money. With few exceptions, so are two or three mailings. Instead, set up a schedule of mailings, four to six weeks apart (too close is irritating and too far apart lets the man forget one mailing before he receives the next), then stick to it. Use a number of different mailing pieces, but keep their appearance and "pitch" closely related. A campaign of three pieces, mailed in 1, 2, 3, order is highly productive. For further visual impact, change the printing colors. If the printing is only one color, vary the colors of ink and paper. In these ways the mailings look different—but difference is not as important as constancy; perseverance is the secret.

TRADE SHOWS

For trade shows, the best inspiration is to attend a few, looking critically at the exhibits, the way firms display their products, and the methods and manners of the booth personnel. Do not be surprised by a wide range of expertise—as with other forms of promotion, the average effectiveness is quite low. Most of the exhibitors are there because they think they should be, because it is an excuse for socializing, or because competitive exhibits force their presence. These defeatist attitudes show up in the booth. Yet many aggressive firms will be at a trade show—with their products prominently displayed and often being demonstrated, with the booth personnel on their toes (both figuratively and literally), and working to make sales. And sales can be made at a trade show—a successful exhibitor can write an astonishing volume of business if he has a good product and presents it properly. Trade shows are expensive and hard work, so if you exhibit, make it pay. A trade show is the best possible way of presenting a new product to a very large number of people in a short period of time.

EDUCATION

Education and selling are practically synonymous. If a prospect knows enough about your new product to believe that owning it will save or make him money, then he will buy it. But he must learn enough about it to erase his natural distrust of the unknown. In industrial purchasing, very seldom is only one man involved. Usually, a number of men must agree before anything new is purchased—and the man with the final decision-making authority often cannot be reached by the salesman. Your only influence at his desk is your reputation and your advertising material. So all of your advertising must have strong educational undertones—and the literature should be deliberately educational. Further, if the product or its proper application is of any complexity, you should create supplementary educational data sheets, manuals, etc. Do not print these in small quantities and meter them out grudgingly—a truly useful operator's manual is more valuable in obtaining sales than a pretty brochure.

The technical copy for educational material will be based upon interviews with someone in engineering—but do not let an engineer write it. First, it will take him forever. Second, he will write it from his own viewpoint, not that of the customer, whose technical grasp of the subject is infinitely lower—perhaps beyond the understanding of the engineer. Instead, have the copy written by an outsider and rewritten until the engineer approves. In this way, technical data is prepared which the customer can understand and use. Tell the customer when/where/how to use it—and how to stay out of trouble. The customer is ignorant—not stupid. He knows that he will have difficulties with an unfamiliar product. So include an intelligent troubleshooting section. Anticipating problems that the customer might have, and showing him how to diagnose and correct them, allays his suspicions in this direction. Without such troubleshooting data, he knows that he is out on the limb when trouble occurs—and he knows that it will.

Most companies overlook this vital information area. In their brochures they give sales features, application data, and specifications for a product, but neglect its innerworkings or how to service it. Therefore, having solid educational material puts you ahead of most competitors—a definite plus. For this reason, stress its availability in your advertising. A definite side benefit of having educational material is that it helps train your own sales force and your distributors. These people are interested in the new product—but busy with other things, they forget most of what they learn during sales presentations. Good technical data lets them hold their own refresher courses.

PERSISTENCE PAYS

It has been said that only 10% of salesmen will make five or more repeat calls on a prospect—and in doing so land 80% of all new customers. This is perseverance—and it applies to advertising too, since the primary purpose is to help gain new customers. All too often, an advertising campaign for a new product starts out with a bang, then everyone hovers over the inquiries—becoming panic stricken because it takes so long to get started. This leads to changes-of-mind, budget cuts, and the campaign is emasculated long before it could become effective.

Do not permit this to happen. As shown in Figure 14-1, any attempt to analyze results, or to correlate advertising inquiries or returns against either cost or ultimate sales will be detrimental unless enough time has elapsed for the campaign to become productive. When the campaign is a year old, it has been in operation long enough to warrant review of its performance and to make *minor* adjustments for the second-year campaign. However, remember that the master plan ran for 2, 3, or more years. Given enough time, advertising is an extremely powerful selling tool. But it does not bring overnight results—and any attempt to evaluate its short-term accomplishments will be self defeating.

Ideas Worth Exploring--No. 13

"ADJUSTABLE" SPACERS FOR ARBOR TOOLS

Description: Split milling-machine arbor spacers, retained on the arbor by fitting into cup spacers adjacent to milling cutters, slitter knives, etc. To change cutter spacing, the arbor nut is loosened a turn or two and the split spacer outside the outboard cutter is removed. Then the cutter is moved over and the split spacer between the cutters is removed and replaced by one of the desired length. A second set of spacers, selected so that the total length of the new spacers is the same as that of the pair removed, is put outside the cutters. The arbor nut is tightened and the changeover is complete. Total time would only be a minute or so since nothing is removed from the arbor by coming off the end—the overarm support, arbor nut, and other spacers all remain in place.

The split spacers and cup spacers should be hardened, precision ground, and marked with their effective length. The rim of the cup spacer could be very shallow (1/32 inch), just enough to hold the two pieces of the split spacer in position.

History: Developed by the author in the early '60s. Used internally—no attempt made to market it.

Marketing Comments: In straddle milling short or medium runs of various part widths, setup time often totals more hours than the cutting time, since the arbor is taken down to change the cutter spacing. The same problem occurs in gang milling (multiple cutters on the arbor), slitting machines for sheet metal, plastic, or paper, and other machines where a tool must be relocated on its arbor or mandrel.

These spacers greatly speed any change over where the same cutters are used. Any firm now making milling machine arbors and spacers, slitting machines, milling cutters, slitting knives, or related tools should find a market for split spacers. Naturally, firms selling the disposable cutter or knife would have the best access to prospects, since their distributors would know the users of the tools.

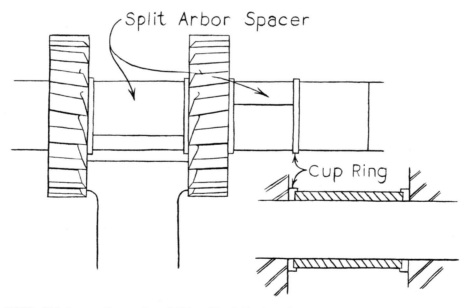

NOTE: This is one of a number of "Ideas Worth Exploring" presented in this book. The author *has not* done this exploring. If a patent is known, it is listed. No listing does *not* mean that the idea is unpatented, or that it can be legally used in any way. Most good ideas have been patented, at one time or another. Most patents have expired and many current ones could probably be contested if literature research turned up prior exposure, as would certainly be the case with many ideas, particularly in the older fields, such as mechanical. *Nevertheless,* none of the ideas given in this book are represented as being free of patents—and the author accepts no responsibility or liability from the use of any of these ideas.

Chapter 15
The Kick-Off

> ... the public birth of a new product should be the first step
> to a profitable future—and it will be, if the introduction is
> done properly and if it occurs when the product is ready for
> it, rather than just because the calendar says "today is the big
> day!" This chapter tells how to make certain that the new
> product is ready to leave the nest and how to build enthusi-
> asm for it among the sales staff and across the distribution
> channels.

YOU CAN WRECK IT NOW

There are three efficient ways of killing a new product. One, do not introduce it formally at all. Two, commence accepting orders before the initial inventory is ready. Three, hold off the introduction until some more convenient time (yet let orders slip through the sales department), thus making the introduction completely anti-climactic.

A properly timed introduction of the new product to the salesmen and distributors is part of the master plan. Keep it that way.

INTRODUCTION TO THE SALESMEN

The kick-off for a new product is a sales meeting—and the salesmen have been to meetings before. To hold their interest and create enthusiasm. the meeting must be a judicious blend of practical facts, selling, and showmanship. If you lean too much on any of the three, the introduction is a flop. Too many facts, delivered in pendantic schoolmaster fashion, will put the salesmen to sleep. A salesman is an ambitious, self-winding, people-oriented man. He must become enthusiastic about the product before trying to sell it—and that means he needs facts. But this enthusiasm is difficult

185

to generate from a dry monotone spooning. On the other hand, don't let the meeting degenerate into a rah-rah spiel or a time-wasting bit of puffery.

The ideal is a largely straightforward technical presentation, but delivered with a dishing of humor and with some showmanship thrown in. Do not have one man carry the show alone. Have at least one man per hour of total length—with none talking longer than a half hour at one time—preferably less. One of the best speakers is an engineer or technical type whom the salesmen know and respect, yet who does field work, understands selling problems, and can think from the salesman's viewpoint.

One of the big mistakes in making sales presentations is to sweep problems under the carpet and hope that the salesmen will not find them. Forget it—they will be the first to find out, so keep all the cards on the table.

The presentation should include (preferably in this order) the new product, what it is, what it is for, and how to use it, who uses it—the type of prospects, type of people now using it (if it is competitive to an existing product), and how to find and identify specific prospects. At this point, have lists of target prospects handed out to each man. These should be the prime prospects only—and not over a dozen firms per man. With these short lists before them, the men can keep their prospects in mind as the rest of the meeting progresses.

Then get into hard details of applying and selling the product—how a customer uses it, how the salesman helps the customer select between the different types and sizes available, the accessories or conditions necessary for proper use, what the salesman needs to know in order to close the sale, trial and service policies, etc.

Hand out samples of the new literature, direct-mail materials, technical and instruction manuals, etc. Do this just before a break, so the salesmen can glance through the material, but the tempo of the meeting is not fouled up by having their attention distracted. After the break, lead them on a page-by-page trip through the literature, showing them where to find the information they may need. Lack of familiarity with sales literature is too frequently seen; it leaves the salesman on one leg.

Move on to a detailed analysis of competitive products. Do not forget alternate products for the same application. It is foolhardy to send the salesmen out into the field without complete knowledge of their competition—including both its strengths and weaknesses. Then return to your own product, going over the sales features again, but in considerable detail, comparing each with competitive sales features and explaining the differences in terms of customer benefits. Go over pricing and delivery—and how this compares with competition. Then go into the technical details of troubleshooting, poor applications, etc. From here, shift back to sales and growth potential, and the fast-growth program. End by concentrating on the prospect lists given out earlier, and what action you want taken during the next 90 days.

A meeting put on in this order sends the salesman back to his territory with a complete working knowledge of the product, how to sell it—where, when, to whom, and how to keep out of trouble. But don't play games—no product in the world is so perfect that the salesmen will not encounter some problems. The more prepared the salesman is, the better off everyone will be.

SHOWING IT TO THE DISTRIBUTORS

No two companies agree on how to introduce a new product to their distributors. Most of them do a poor job—a major contributing factor to the frequency of new product flops. The commonest and probably least successful arrangement is to leave all distributor presentations up to the salesmen. Don't—you send a relatively ignorant but mildly interested salesman (from a one-day school) out to talk to completely ignorant and mostly disinterested distributor salesmen. This just guarantees that any presentations made at the prospect's desk will be as emasculated and erroneous as possible.

On the opposite end of the spectrum would be attempting to pull all the distributors together for a mass presentation. This is probably impractical, because of their sheer numbers and the travel expenses involved. The most effective compromise is a regional (city) gathering of distributor personnel, if this is possible. If not, then you have no solution except to plan on major presentations to the leading distributors individually. A presentation team can cover four or five distributors a week—twice that many if they are close together. At the end of a month you can hit 20 or 30 distributors across the country. This is enough to get the ball rolling.

Have two salesmen at each meeting—the one from that territory and the other from an adjacent one. They are there to help—and to learn, so that they can join forces to put on additional presentations to lesser distributors after learning how to do it.

Do not let any presentation take more than two hours, preferably one. If the meeting takes over an hour, break it in the middle. The meeting is started by the new-product staff man, then turned over to the out-of-territory salesman to describe the product and its features. The territory salesman then takes over, to talk about applications and prospects. The session wraps up with the second headquarters man discussing specifications, prices, and delivery. A brief question/answer period trails the formal presentation.

When properly managed, the distributor salesmen have a feel for the product and what to do with it. They know that their local factory salesman is familiar with the product and can give them help when needed. Most important, the presentation has tied in with local conditions, local prospects, and local competitive situations. The distributor salesmen will bring in purchase orders and turn up prospects for the firm's salesman to follow. The stage is set for building profitable volume.

Ideas Worth Exploring--No. 14

PRESS LOADER/UNLOADER

Description: A pneumatically operated press loader/unloader, controlled by limit switches actuated by the ram movement. While the ram is down, the device waits in the outward position, with the load/unload arm in its up position. As the ram goes up, it trips a limit switch and the in/out cylinder pulls the device toward the press, so that the arm reaches inside the die space. Then the up/down cylinder forces the arm downward onto the stamping. Cups are pressed against the work and the vacuum/blow cylinder is moved to its outward position, creating a mild vacuum within the cylinder, hollow arms, and the cups. Alternate lifting devices could be employed, such as electromagnets.

The up/down cylinder then lifts the arm and the stamping free of the die and the device is forced outward by the in/out cylinder. With the device in the outward position, the vacuum/blow cylinder is reversed and the work is blown free of the cups. When used as a loader, the vacuum/blow cylinder cycling is reversed. A pair of such devices can automatically load and unload a press.

The design could be developed to suit any press using forming or drawing dies. Between electromagnets and contoured cups, stampings of any shape could be handled. By equipping the arm with multiple cups, stampings of large size and practically any weight could be sucessfully handled. The unit is fail safe—the toggle arrangement automatically ejects the unloader arms from the die space if the limit-switch system should fail or the ram descend while the unloader was inside the press.

History: A device somewhat similar to this was designed and patented by one Charles Hayward in 1955—Patent No. 2,867,185. A number of the units were made and used by his employer but the device was not marketed.

Marketing Comments: The design offers interesting possibilities. Grasping unloaders cannot unload finished stampings because they cause mutilation. Precoated, painted, or similar stock is usually eliminated because the work is dragged across the die. Normally grasping tabs are left on the work—but these then require a subsequent trimming operation. While "transfer" devices bypass this problem, they are relatively slow and complex considering the light weight of the workpiece.

The device shown has neither of these limitations, and should be lower in cost. The total market potential is substantial—and probably could be broadened by extending the device to other types of equipment—plastic molding and vacuum forming, laminating presses, etc.

Where to Look: Examine the Hayward patent, and make a routine search for similar patents.

NOTE: This is one of a number of "Ideas Worth Exploring" presented in this book. The author *has not* done this exploring. If a patent is known, it is listed. No listing does *not* mean that the idea is unpatented, or that it can be legally used in any way. Most good ideas have been patented, at one time or another. Most patents have expired and many current ones could probably be contested if literature research turned up prior exposure, as would certainly be the case with many ideas, particularly in the older fields, such as mechanical. *Nevertheless,* none of the ideas given in this book are represented as being free of patents—and the author accepts no responsibility or liability from the use of any of these ideas.

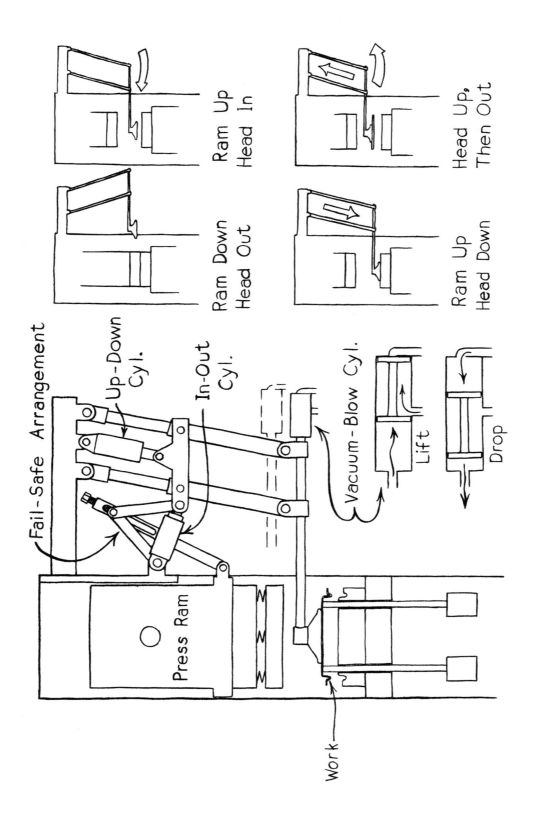

Ram Up
Head In

Head Up,
Then Out

Ram Down
Head Out

Ram Up
Head Down

Fail-Safe Arrangement

Up-Down Cyl.

In-Out Cyl.

Press Ram

Vacuum-Blow Cyl.

Lift

Drop

Work

Chapter 16
Selling That Gets Results

> . . . the new-product department's job does not end with the product's introduction: in a very real sense, the vital part is just beginning, because the objective is not to create new products—but to build profitable ones. The difference comes in the first few years of selling—and this chapter tells how the new-product development group works with sales, building volume during the new product's adolescent stage until it has achieved volume, penetration, and profits that permit turning it over to routine selling.

YOU HAVE TO GET INVOLVED

Over a period of many years, routine sales of a new product may produce worthwhile sales volume—but it is not likely. Salesmen are paid a commission against sales, work against a quota, or some combination of these two. They divide their time between customers, prospects, and the company's products on a basis that provides them with the greatest income; staying away from products that are difficult to sell or which get them in trouble, and concentrating on products which are good "movers."

While every salesman knows that he must develop prospects, the plain fact is that he has almost no time in which to do this. He may have a handful of prospects that he is working on, but he cannot chase smokestacks—even if he wants to.

Therefore, if sales of a new product are to build rapidly, somebody has to provide an extracurricular effort. Without hiring more men, the sales department cannot do this. Since the extra effort is only needed for a short period—3 to 5 years, the best idea is to have one or more salesmen types on the new-product department staff (or new product types in the sales department). Their job is to work with the salesmen but to push only the new product, finding and developing prospects and pushing sales to the point where the product can be turned over to the salesman. This may be a difficult concept to sell management. However, if the company is spending a large sum on new product development, it is foolhardy to deny the necessity of having salesmen on the new-product department staff. (In a very small firm the "salesman" might be the new-product manager.)

The only potential difficulty is friction between the short-term salesman and the regular salesman in a territory. This can best be offset by having the former salaried, with the regular salesman drawing full commission on all sales in his area. Further, the new-product salesman should assist the regular salesmen when calling on established customers and prospects, but devote most of his time to prospects whom the regular man does not sell.

Some companies may turn thumbs down on the idea of the new-product salesmen working independently of the regular men. However, these are home-office concepts which can be largely ignored in the field. The actual working methods must be tailored to each area salesman. Some will grasp the concept and appreciate the new-product sales efforts. Others, preoccupied by jealousy, nest-building, insecurity, or frightened to death of having a home-office man call on a prospect when he is not present, will put up a stiff resistance. It is self-evident that the primary prospects must be in territories served by cooperative salesmen—because prospects in areas served by non-cooperative salesmen must be considered as secondary.

AN ORDINARY MAN AWAY FROM HOME

Territory management is a delicate thing. It depends to a small degree upon the firm's reputation, and to a greater degree upon the company's products, delivery, and prices. But most of all it depends upon the delicate interplay between the salesman and the people in the customer's purchasing, engineering, and operating areas. The new-product salesman must enhance this relationship, but only in the sense of helping the salesman obtain orders for the new product and then keeping the customers happy. He must be extremely careful not to apply undue pressure or to thrust the new product into conversations involving routine products or selling—in short, to speak when invited to do so.

During an hour's conversation with a customer, the new product may not be mentioned at all. It may be given only passing attention, or the customer may be actively interested and half or more of the meeting may be devoted to it. There will be no red carpets rolled out. The customer is as likely to greet the new product salesman by complaining bitterly about some routine matter as he is to sweep his desk clean for a serious discussion of a new product.

Further, the new-product man must stick to the one thing that he is authorized to talk about—the new product. Nothing more. He must bend over backwards to avoid participating in any conversation concerning the company's existing products, policies, quality, delivery, price, competitors, etc. He is in the customer's presence for only one purpose. By moving a fraction of an inch past that line, he not only defeats his purpose but can cause irrevocable harm.

WHAT NEEDS FIXING?

A large part of the new-product field work will be in service or customer followup. These are vital. It is most important that the new-product man (manager) see the product in use, and get the customer's reactions to pricing, delivery, functions, advantages and disadvantages, application or servicing problems, etc. Although the new product is now in production, it does not mean that the design cannot be altered or improved.

Customer feedback yields ideas for advertising and future sales pitches. It also reveals problems, which must be examined carefully. It may be customer ignorance, indicating faults or omissions in the sales literature and instruction materials. If complaints are scattered, with no real concentration, no correction may be needed unless the quantity is large. But if a pattern establishes itself, such as frequent complaints about the location of the switches, or the packaging, or any of a million other things, then serious attention is necessary.

PATCHING THE WEAK SPOTS

If the new product has weaknesses, they must be corrected. In spite of extensive market research, field testing, and in-plant experience, if it is humanly possible to have problems with the product, customers will do it. Expect it.

While nothing can ever be foolproof, a new product should be fool resistant. If it is not, then the troublesome aspect must be isolated. But at all costs, do not make hasty decisions about design changes. Often a simple change snowballs into a real mess, making advertising erroneous, forcing quickie tooling which malfunctions at leisure, fouling up production scheduling and operations, and making existing inventory obsolete. Make necessary changes—but make them slowly, thoughtfully, thoroughly, and only after calm deliberation.

THE MATURE LOOK AHEAD

A year after the product's introduction, you can see how well it is doing. Sooner than that is too early. But the new-product manager has been keeping tally on the sales volume, returns, service problems, etc. If minor corrections were necessary, they have been made. If a major miscalculation was found, it may have been necessary to shut down the entire operation while repairs were made. This should not have happened if the product was properly planned and developed. But pencils have erasers; the best-laid plans do sometimes go astray and on occasion it is necessary to stop, correct, regroup, and then start over.

When the original sales forecast was made, it was based upon a mountain of guesses and next to no actual facts. As each month passes, the mountain of guesses shrinks and the molehill of facts assumes tangible shape. Within six months the sales forecast can be reshaped in the light of actuality. By the end of the first year, the new-product manager knows how things are going and his projection for the next few years should be quite accurate.

It is unfortunate that we humans tend to learn only from our mistakes—very seldom from our successes. If the new product fares worse than expected, everybody scrambles to fix it and get it on the projected sales curve. But if it goes up the sales curve more readily than expected, the natural inclination is to sit back, relax, and enjoy success. This is fine for weekends. But come Monday morning, be back in there guaranteeing that the success is self-perpetuating. The new product will not build itself; that which goes up can come down unless sales volume is deliberately pushed ever higher. At all costs do not scrap the long-term plan, or cut a few years off the intensive-care period.

Do not forget that competitors are watching every move. It if looks as though you have a good thing, they are laying serious plans to join you. It is not at all unusual to find a company introduce a product, enjoy a tremendous success for the first year or so, relax while sales build upwards automatically—then wake up one morning to find sales drooping because competitors have jumped into the market. Nothing but long-term hard work can push a new product up to significant penetration of the available market—and keep it there.

PLANNING THE EXIT

By the beginning of the third year, the new-product manager and the sales manager should begin to plan the exit of the new-product department's sales activity and turning the new product over to routine sales management. In doing this, resurvey the original list of primary and secondary prospects and find out which ones have not yet become customers. The last year is an ideal opportunity to concentrate heavily on adding this original group of key prospects to the customer list. Tackle the knotty problems: stubborn prospects, customers who bought the product and threw it out, and other maintenance and repair work for the salesmen. In this way, the new-product department exits knowing that they accomplished what they set out to do and left no dirty laundry or unfinished business in the field. With this taken care of, the salesmen can carry the ball for the future.

ONE THING AT A TIME

By this time, it should be apparent that the successful development and marketing of a new product demands a tremendous amount of work and singleness of purpose from a number of people over a number of years. There is no such thing as an overnight success. For this reason, it is foolhardy to expect the average company to maintain this effort for more than one product at a time. It might be possible internally, but in the field it poses insurmountable problems.

At the introductory kick-off meeting you should talk about one product and one product only. Furthermore, you should not have another meeting a month later for a second new product. By that time, most salesmen are just getting comfortable when thinking about the first one. Two products introduced close together cancel out each other. Half the salesmen will drop the first ball (which they have not picked up yet anyway) and concentrate on the second one. The other half have become interested in the first one and thus have no time left over for the second product. A rapid succession of new products can only be successful in the aggregate—analyzed individually, each will miss projections by a wide margin.

KEEPING ALL THE IRONS HOT

However, you need not wait until one product achieves full maturity before starting the next—just phase them six months to a year apart. This scheduling gives adequate time to do a thorough job on each stage of one project, before shifting to the next. Each department involved in new-product development keeps involved—but does have a breather between them. Of course, products spaced 6 to 12 months apart will overlap during the sales effort, so the actual timing is more a matter of the size of the new-product sales group than any other factor—except the firm's ability to finance rapid growth. When possible, develop a product which is salable to the same market as its immediate predecessor. In this way, the primary prospects for the new product are people who have already been contacted, and may be satisfied customers for the earlier product. By judicious planning of sequential new-product introduction, the entire sales procedure becomes more efficient and more profitable.

The key to success is the word "profit." Assuring it requires forethought and planning. One of the best ways to capitalize on planning is to do a thorough job in one market at a time—becoming all things to a few people, rather than a few things to all people.

BIBLIOGRAPHY

Basic Checklist and Idea Book for Advertising, Marketing, Sales Executives. Printers' Ink Publishing Corp., 635 Madison Avenue, New York 10022. (A great deal of this book is devoted to marketing of consumer products. However, it is an excellent source of ideas and checklists for the neophyte new-product manager because of its extensive coverage of all promotion tools—including some which may not be familiar to his firm's advertising department.)

Developing a Product Strategy: Planning, Production, Promotion. No. 39 in the AMA Management Report Series. American Management Association, 1515 Broadway, Times Square, New York 10036. (An older text, published in 1959. It is an anthology of articles written by a number of individuals. Much of the material is consumer oriented, but there are some valuable idea provokers.)

Handbook of New Product Development, P. Hilton. Prentice-Hall, Inc., Englewood Cliffs, New Jersey. (Presents a solid program which highlights planning, budgeting, financing, researching, and testing of new products. Replete with fascinating case studies.)

How to Succeed in Business Without Really Trying, Shepherd Mead. Simon and Schuster, Inc., New York. (An indispensable manual for the neophyte manager of anything.)

Industrial Marketing, August 1965. Crain Communications Inc., 740 Rush Street, Chicago, Illinois 60611. (An issue devoted to marketing research; of interest because of the breadth of experiences and suggestions offered.)

Introduction to Operations Research, C. West Churchman, Russell L. Ackoff, and E. Leonard Arnoff. John Wiley & Sons, Inc., New York. (A basic text on analysis of data and on decision making. It will tell you more than you want to know.)

Keeping Old Products New, P. Hilton. Prentice-Hall, Inc., Englewood Cliffs, New Jersey. (Contains proven strategies that can result in new streams of earnings from established products.)

New Decision-Making Tools for Managers, Edward C. Bursk and John F. Chapman. Harvard University Press, reprinted by The New American Library, Inc., as a Mentor Executive Library Book, 1963. (This is a valuable and fascinating book. However, most of the suggestions can be enacted only at top management level. For the neophyte, it shows him what might be—which is often frustrating.)

New Product Planning, A Practical Guide to Diversification, H. Watton. Prentice-Hall, Inc., Englewood Cliffs, New Jersey. (Step-by-step procedures showing how a new-product program can be established so it achieves corporate goals.)

'New Products: Are We Organized for Them?" Hector Lazo, *Industrial Marketing,* December, 1963, and "Marketing," Hector Lazo, *Industrial Marketing,* November, 1963. Crain Communications, Inc., 740 Rush Street, Chicago, Illinois 60611. (These two articles give interesting analyses of the organization of new-product development in various companies.)

Parkinson's Law—Or the Pursuit of Progress, C. Northcote Parkinson. John Murray, London, 1957. (This book makes clear many of the aspects of corporate management which appear obscure to the junior—or even the senior—executive. It is, perhaps, couched in unnecessarily technical language.)

Sales Forecasting: Uses, Techniques, and Trends, American Management Association Special Report No. 16. American Management Association, 1515 Broadway, Times Square, New York 10036. (Thirteen articles by different individuals, plus a survey appendix.)

Statistical Sales Forecasting, Vernon G. Lippitt. Financial Executives Institute, 50 W. 44th Street, New York 10036. 1969. (A basic text on the fine art of sales forecasting.)

The Art and Craft of Moving Executive Mountains, Henry M. Boettinger. *Business Management,* July, August, September 1969. 22 West Putnam Avenue, Greenwich, Connecticut 06830. (An interesting and only slightly tongue-in-cheek handbook on how to get upper management to move.)

The New Product, Delmar W. Karger. The Industrial Press, 93 Worth Street, New York 10013. (A basic text on consumer new-product development in major companies. Interesting and valuable for its many checklists and realistic approach.)

The Peter Principle, Laurence F. Peter and Raymond Hull. William Morrow & Co., Inc., New York. (A piercing investigation into the structure of the organization. Not recommended for the neophyte—but of absorbing interest and usefulness for the elderly junior executive.)

The Profitable Product: Its Planning, Launching, and Management, W. Talley. Prentice-Hall, Inc., Englewood Cliffs, New Jersey. (Breaks subject down in two elements, goals and strategies, and treats both in four dimensions—market, distribution channel, selling effort, and product.)

Three-Upmanship, Stephen Potter. Holt, Rinehart and Winston, New York. (A guide to human relations. Particularly useful in developing working arrangements with department heads and with subordinates.)

Index

P